What Should We Expect of Family Literacy?

Experiences of Latino Children Whose Parents Participate in an Intergenerational Literacy Project

What Should We Expect of Family Literacy?

Experiences of Latino Children Whose Parents Participate in an Intergenerational Literacy Project

Jeanne R. Paratore

Boston University
Boston, Massachusetts, USA

Gigliana Melzi

New York University
New York, New York, USA

Barbara Krol-Sinclair

Chelsea, Massachusetts Public Schools
Chelsea, Massachusetts, USA

INTERNATIONAL
Reading
Association

800 Barksdale Road
PO Box 8139
Newark, Delaware 19714-8139, USA
www.reading.org

NATIONAL READING CONFERENCE

National Reading Conference
122 South Michigan Avenue
Suite 1100
Chicago, Illinois 60603, USA

Copyright 1999 by the International Reading Association, Inc., and the National Reading Conference.

The International Reading Association attempts, through its publications, to provide a forum for a wide spectrum of opinions on reading. This policy permits divergent viewpoints without implying the endorsement of the Association.

Library of Congress Cataloging in Publication Data
      Paratore, Jeanne R.
      What should we expect of family literacy? Experiences of Latino children whose parents participate in an intergenerational literacy project / Jeanne R. Paratore, Gigliana Melzi, Barbara Krol-Sinclair.
          p.   cm.—(Literacy studies series)
      Includes bibliographical references and index.
      1. Family literacy programs—United States—Case studies.   2. Reading—Parent participation—United States—Case studies.   3. English language—Study and teaching—United States—Spanish speakers—Case studies.   4. Hispanic American children—Education (Elementary)—Case studies.   5. Children of immigrants—Education (Elementary)—United States—Case studies.   6. Education, Bilingual—United States—Case studies.   I. Melzi, Gigliana.   II. Krol-Sinclair, Barbara.   III. Title.   IV. Series.
LC151.P37   1999   98-53892
372.119'2—dc21
ISBN 0-87207-246-0
Printed in Canada

Contents

Note From the Series Editors

Jeanne Paratore, Gigliana Melzi, and Barbara Krol-Sinclair ask and answer a very important question: What should we expect of family literacy? Their premise that every parent cares deeply about the literacy development of their children regardless of their wealth, poverty, or educational achievements sets the positive tone for this volume. Through their 10 years of work with the Chelsea Project, a cooperative partnership between Boston University and the Chelsea, Massachusetts Public Schools, the authors have rejoiced with hundreds of parents and children who have been involved with their family literacy project. The results of this project are presented objectively in this important volume and will serve to enlighten researchers and educators who are planning family literacy programs. This volume promises to become a mandatory book for all family literacy educators and advocates.

We hope that this excellent volume will serve as a reference tool as educators plan literacy programs for learners of all ages and cultures. This book as well as others in the Literacy Studies Series broadens our understanding of research and provides guidance as we design our instructional practices. The goal of the Series is to advance knowledge in the literacy field and to help make research a more important focus in the literacy community. The volumes in this Series are intended to inform literacy instruction and research by reporting findings from state-of-the-art literacy endeavors. We believe that this text successfully accomplishes this goal.

James Flood
Diane Lapp
Series Editors
San Diego State University
San Diego, California, USA

Review Board

Dr. Nancy C. Padak
Kent State University
Kent, Ohio

Dr. Jeanne R. Paratore
Boston University
Boston, Massachusetts

Dr. Victoria Purcell-Gates
Harvard University
Cambridge, Massachusetts

Dr. Nancy L. Roser
University of Texas at Austin
Austin, Texas

Dr. Diane L. Schallert
University of Texas at Austin
Austin, Texas

Dr. Lyndon W. Searfoss
Arizona State University
Tucson, Arizona

Dr. Peter N. Winograd
University of New Mexico
Albuquerque, New Mexico

Dr. M. Jo Worthy
University of Texas at Austin
Austin, Texas

Foreword

The issue of diversity in schools is certainly not new. For many years, public schools have had to face the racial, cultural, or class differences of the children who enroll in their programs. What seems to be new, however, is the response to these differences by some educators who seek to turn the diversity of students into assets for their schooling. Heretofore, the most common response to diversity, at least in schools within the United States, and undoubtedly elsewhere as well, has been to eradicate it, to strip it away, to erase it, to practice what educational historian Joel Spring (1997) has called "deculturalization." This practice, which forms part of a broader and pervasive ideology with a long history in the United States, is still prevalent today, especially given the rapid demographic shifts in society, witness the deplorable language policies being implemented in California under the guise of helping children learn English.

The demographic reality remains, however, that the so-called "language minority" students are now the majority in most, if not all, of the major urban school districts in the United States, leading to the awkward and revealing term of "minority-majority" schools and districts. The issue of how to address diversity in schools, therefore, promises to be the foremost educational issue well into the 21st century. In fact, in my estimation, educational researchers who do not address issues of diversity in one form or another, especially in the United States, are at risk of their work becoming irrelevant. This risk of irrelevance does not seem to matter, however; the overwhelming majority of studies about educational change still do not address the education of language minority students or issues of schools serving such students. Deculturalization, therefore, is not only a standard educational practice and the dominant ideology, but seems to be the norm in educational (and psychological) research as well.

In this context, this new book by Jeanne Paratore, Gigliana Melzi, and Barbara Krol-Sinclair, reporting their literacy research with Latino families and students, and done in collaboration with teachers, is not only a welcomed contribution, insightful and informative, but a breath of fresh air. In these pages you will learn about their family literacy project, not one that offers ethnocentric and simplistic prescriptions to families, as is often the norm, but one that attempts to understand and accommodate the parents' and students' experiences and knowledge on their own terms, while offering ideas and resources of assistance to the families and their children in regard to school learning. Although these authors recognize, and it comes across clearly in this well-written and highly readable book, that the term *Latino* belies enormous diversity of history and life experiences, they also point out what by now is well documented but bears repeating: These families value education very highly and hold high aspirations for their children. In fact, Latino working-class families have a strong faith in schools, which educators should recognize as an obvious asset. However, this faith may be misplaced given dominant ideologies and the social stratification of schooling, and it often contrasts sharply with what many teachers believe (as reported by the authors) and with the hypercritical (and vigilant) attitude of middle-class families toward schools.

I would like to offer three other points that also characterize this book, and that I have found to be central elements in working with Latino families (for example, Moll & González, 1997; Mercado & Moll, 1997). One is that to acknowledge the diversity of "lived experiences" among Latinos (or among any other group), one must move away from the more "normative" models of culture, with their static traits and attributes, toward cultural approaches that highlight the particularities of experiences—"la cultura vivida" as we say in Spanish—how people live culturally, using resources of all kinds to cope with their material conditions of life.

A second point, which the authors of this book do so well, is to approach the families and students with the respect they merit and deserve. One strategy is not to assume that, as educators, we can only teach the families about how to do school, but that we can learn valuable lessons by coming to know the families, by taking the time to establish the social relationships necessary to create personal links between households and classrooms. It is through these social relationships, of necessity reciprocal in nature, that the social capital of both families and teachers is fostered and developed.

Finally, as the authors emphasize in presenting their analysis of successful and not-so-successful cases, the complexities of schools and of life make such projects quite fragile. No family literacy project, as they point out, regardless of good intentions and design, may compensate for a low-level intellectual curriculum, or for reductionist teaching practices, or for the thinly veiled racist and political attacks on Latino families and their children. But our responsibility as educators, I am sure the authors would agree, is to continue to work with integrity and with passion in facilitating resources that may make a positive difference for the families and children in our studies. And as such, I congratulate them on their fine work.

Luis C. Moll
University of Arizona
Tucson, Arizona, USA

References

Mercado, C., & Moll, L.C. (1997). The study of funds of knowledge: Collaborative research in Latino homes. *Centro*, 9(9), 26–42.

Moll, L.C., & González, N. (1997). Teachers as social scientists: Learning about culture from household research. In P.M. Hall (Ed.), *Race, ethnicity and multiculturalism* (pp. 89–114). New York: Garland.

Spring, J. (1997). *Deculturalization and the struggle for equality* (2nd ed.). New York: McGraw-Hill.

Acknowledgments

We wish to thank the children, parents, and teachers who worked with us to help us understand the children's home and school literacies. We are also grateful to the following graduate students for their research assistance: Cassandra Brown, Katherine Stankard Ha, Francisco Hernández, Cristina Pérez, Jane Jackson, and Francesca Pomerantz.

CHAPTER 1

What Have We Learned About Family Literacy? An Introduction

During the last several years, family literacy programs have been the focus of substantial interest and attention as a solution to the problem of underachievement by so many children in our schools. Increasingly, educational dollars are allotted to programs that serve family units, rather than parents and children individually. The recent reauthorization of Title I (a federally funded program in the United States intended to help disadvantaged children who may be at risk of school failure), for example, increases a school's responsibility to offer services to both parents and children and identifies as a priority programs that connect adult, early childhood, and elementary education. Legislation currently pending in the U.S. Congress (Reading Excellence Act, 1998) will, if authorized, provide funding for programs based on the Even Start model (a federally funded program in the United States for delivering literacy services to parents and children) that "enable parents to be their child's first and most important teacher" (p. 4). In adult education, it is now common for funding guidelines to require that programs provide adult participants access to instruction in family literacy.

Family literacy initiatives that are supported by such funding opportunities have met with mixed response. On one side, they are viewed as holding the key to eventual academic success of children who are identified as at risk for failure in U.S. schools. This view is based primarily on findings related to three areas of research. First, book-reading experiences during early childhood have correlated strongly with eventual success in reading (Cochran-Smith, 1983; Durkin, 1966; Teale, 1986), leading experts to conclude that preparing parents to read to children on a regular basis would support children's school success. Second, programs that involve parents in their children's education have been found to have a positive influence on children's cognitive development and academic performance (Bronfenbrenner, 1974; Henderson & Berla, 1994; Kellaghan, Sloane, Alvarez, & Bloom, 1993). Third, children's academic achievement has correlated highly with levels of parental education (Applebee, Langer, & Mullis, 1988; Sticht & McDonald, 1990).

An early voice in the study of the intergenerational transfer of literacy, Sticht (1992) noted that children who arrive at kindergarten well behind their peers are often the same children who fall behind quickly in school and eventually drop out. He explained that these same students eventually

> become parents of children and are unable to transmit educationally relevant preschool oral and written language skills, which are the foundation for later reading and writing skills, or to model reasoning and thinking skills, frequently using mathematical concepts. Without these basics in language, numeracy, and critical thinking, the children from these homes show up for school prepared to recapitulate the failure of their parents, and the cycle repeats itself. (p. 1)

The influence of this viewpoint is evident in the design of many family literacy programs. In describing the philosophy underlying the programs sponsored by the National Center for Family Literacy, Potts and Paull (1995) gave the following explanation:

> The programs are based on the assumption that parents are powerful: Their attitudes convey a critical message about schooling, the work and joy of learning, and the connection between education and quality of life. Most children who succeed in school learned early that reading and learning are important and that educational goals are attainable. But in some families, children absorb very different attitudes concerning what is expected, what is desirable, and what is possible.... Parental messages often reflect their own low self-esteem and limited expectations. The PACE/Kenan programs aim to change those messages; they provide opportunities for parents and other caregivers to develop the

skills and confidence that enable them to see possibilities in place of dead ends. They also offer programs for young children to build social skills and improve their readiness to learn. But they understand that educating parents does not necessarily improve parental interactions with children. PACE/Kenan directors know that educating children might not have long-term effects if the messages in the home do not support their learning, so they offer parent education and groups where adults can learn parenting and life-coping skills and develop a network of friends. They also provide time each day for parents and children to play together, so parents can practice the skills they are learning to support their children's emerging literacy. (pp. 168–169)

On the other side of the debate, family literacy programs are regarded as interventions that interpret family differences as deprivation (for example, Taylor, 1993; Valdés, 1996) and as representative of a belief that children will succeed in schools only if "they are taught to behave in more traditionally mainstream ways in specially designed intervention programs" (Valdés, 1996, p. 17).

Auerbach (1995b) reviewed several family literacy program models and argued that the assumptions underlying such programs were not supported by research. Regarding the assumption that the homes of low-income, minority families are literacy impoverished, she noted that "study after study refutes the notion that poor, minority, and immigrant families do not value or support literacy development" (p. 15). She re-examined the belief that certain ways of using literacy at home better prepare children for success in school and concluded that "studies suggest that the extent to which parents use literacy in socially significant ways as an integral part of family life rather than the extent to which they do intentional, add-on literacy tasks with children is key in shaping children's literacy acquisition" (p. 19). Auerbach also questioned the assumption concerning the relative importance of home and school factors in literacy acquisition and the belief that what happens at home is key to school success. Paraphrasing Heath (1983), she concluded that "it is the schools that need to change to accommodate family and community literacy practices rather than the homes that need to change to support schooling" (p. 20).

Many other researchers have echoed Auerbach's viewpoint. Swadener (1995) commented that existing early intervention programs emphasize "getting the child 'ready' for school, rather than get-

3

ting the school 'ready' to serve increasingly diverse children" (p. 18). Similarly, Valdés (1996) cautioned that those who advocate parent involvement as a way to break the cycle of low achievement are well-intentioned but misguided:

> They are subscribing to existing mythologies about the power of school to right all social wrongs, and they are failing to take into account how social inequalities, educational ideologies, educational structures, and interpersonal interactions work together to affect educational outcomes. (p. 195)

Perhaps the strongest voice on this side of the debate has been that of Taylor (1997), who made the following argument:

> The recent focus on family literacy that is seemingly designed to bring more literacy to parents and children is an effort to shift the blame for poverty and underemployment onto the people least responsible for and least able to struggle against the systematic inequalities of modern societies. (p. 2)

Our Beliefs and Influences

Since we started our work in family literacy in 1989, we have found ourselves squarely in the middle of this debate. At the outset, we were influenced by Lareau's (1989) study of high- and low-income families and their interactions with schools. Of particular interest was her discussion of Bourdieu's (1977) premise that "family life provides resources ('capital') which yield important social profits" (p. 5). Lareau noted that "the standards of the school are not neutral; their requests for parent involvement may be laden with the cultural experiences of intellectual and economic elites" (p. 8), experiences low-income and undereducated families are unlikely to share. She argued that her data provided clear evidence that the differences in the interactions that occurred in the families she studied could be explained largely by differences in what Bourdieu termed *social capital*—familiarity with the diagnostic and instructional language used by teachers, the status to approach teachers as social equals, access to income and material resources, and similarity in style, routine, and purpose of family work. Lareau concluded,

Families may be very similar in how much they stress the importance of education or how frequently and diligently they attempt to teach their children new words, but they may differ in how closely these activities are tied to the school's curriculum, how much they monitor their children's school performance, and how much they complain to educators. (p. 170)

We also were influenced greatly by the often-quoted work of Delpit (1988). In arguing for the need for explicit instruction in literacy for children of color, Delpit explained,

To provide schooling for everyone's children that reflects liberal, middle-class values and aspirations is to ensure the maintenance of the status quo, to ensure that power, the culture of power, remains in the hands of those who already have it. Some children come to school with more accoutrements of the culture of power already in place—"cultural capital," as some critical theorists refer to it—some with less. Many liberal educators hold that the primary goal for education is for children to become autonomous, to develop fully who they are in the classroom setting without having arbitrary, outside standards forced upon them. This is a very reasonable goal for people whose children are already participants in the culture of power and who have already internalized its codes. (p. 285)

As we worked with the immigrant families in our community, it was easy for us to justify our work on the basis of Lareau's and Delpit's comments. Surely, we reasoned, parents who have never attended U.S. schools, who speak a different language, and who have little experience with mainstream culture and values, will benefit from learning more about English language, English literacy, and U.S. schooling.

At the same time, however, we continued to be guided by the work of Taylor and Dorsey-Gaines (1988) who argued forcefully that educators are looking for the explanation for school failure in the wrong place, that it is not the lack of parental knowledge about or support for children's literacy development, but rather the lack of social, political, and economic support for parents in dealing with housing, health, and other social problems that put children at risk.

We have worked from the belief that programs serving immigrant parents who wish to develop their own English literacy and to support their children's success in U.S. schools can be responsive to both these viewpoints: They cannot only teach "the codes needed to participate fully in the mainstream of American life" (Delpit, 1988,

p. 45), but they also can recognize and build on what Moll and Green-berg (1990) referred to as "household funds of knowledge" and de-scribed as "a major, untapped resource for academic instruction" (p. 327). Moll and Greenberg explained that families exist not in isolation but rather in interactive communities where adults and children pos-sess and share specific and diverse funds of knowledge about work life, social life, and school life. These funds of knowledge, they ar-gued, are available in households regardless of the families' years of formal schooling or of the prominence they assign to literacy, and are "central to home life and to the relationship of the families to oth-ers in their community" (p. 323).

There is evidence to support the belief that these two viewpoints could be joined. In her longitudinal study of 10 Mexican families in Carpinteria, California, Delgado-Gaitan (1990, 1994, 1996) found that family literacy classes served to empower parents in several ways: The parents learned more about schools and school literacies and there-fore gained confidence in their interactions with teachers and admin-istrators; as parents and children spent more time reading and writing together, they created a context for sharing values and opinions about the importance of family; and, in cases in which reading with their chil-dren was not a common activity prior to parents' participation in liter-acy classes, parents and children "accepted changes in their family organization to accommodate the new behavior" (1994, p. 167). Shanahan, Mulhern, and Rodriguez-Brown (1995) studied the effects of Project FLAME, a family literacy program whose name was derived from Spanish, the first language of the immigrant families it serves—Family Literacy: Aprendiendo, Mejorando, Educando (Learning, Bet-tering, Educating). They reported that it led to improved English pro-ficiency for parents, improvements in children's knowledge of letter names and print awareness, more frequent visits by parents to school, greater numbers of literacy materials at home, and more confidence in parents' helping with their children's homework. Similarly, Quintero and Huerta-Macías (1990) and Quintero and Velarde (1990) reported that parents and children who participated in Family Initiative for Eng-lish Literacy displayed enhanced opportunities for literacy and biliter-acy development, increased interaction between parents and their chil-dren's teachers, and increased self-confidence of parents in helping their children with their schoolwork. Ada (1988) worked with Spanish-speaking parents to develop children's reading and writing skills through the use of children's literature. She found that parents increased their awareness of their children's strengths and needs in literacy, their understanding of how they are able to support their children's literacy learning, and their own self-confidence in their ability to discuss their children's learning with classroom teachers.

In our own work, we, too, have found and reported evidence that providing parents with opportunities to extend their own literacy and language while learning about ways to support their children in U.S. schools had many positive effects: increased English literacy and language proficiency for parents, increased incidence of shared literacy at home, and increased understandings about classrooms and classroom literacies (Krol-Sinclair, 1996; Paratore, 1993, 1994, 1995).

However, although previous investigations related to our own work and that of others explored the influence of family literacy interventions on parents' developing literacy, on the practice of family literacy, and on the ways such interventions influenced parent-teacher interactions, little has been written about the subsequent school experiences of the children. The research that does exist relies primarily on evaluating children's performance on the basis of test scores (for example, Seaman, Popp, & Darling, 1991). As other researchers have noted (for example, Delgado-Gaitan, 1996; Epstein, 1996), the effects of parent involvement in schooling on children's academic success may not be reflected in short-term or traditional indicators. In an attempt to address this issue, we began our study by extending the definition of school success beyond achievement on large-scale tests. We based our evaluation on a combination of interview and anecdotal data as well as report card, attendance, and retention data.

We posed three questions in our study: (1) In what ways do parents who participate in the Intergenerational Literacy Project (ILP) support their children's academic achievement? (2) In what ways do children of participating parents use literacy at home alone and with their parents? and (3) What is the nature of the school experiences of children whose parents have participated in an intergenerational literacy project? In the chapters that follow, we present our methodology, the children's profiles, and our analysis and interpretation of the results.

CHAPTER 2

The Present Study: Literacy Experiences of Children Whose Parents Participate in an Intergenerational Literacy Project

Setting

The setting for the study was a small, urban community where the majority of families are new immigrants to the United States. In the school population, approximately 60% of the families are Latino, 15% are Southeast Asian, and 25% represent Caucasian and other ethnicities. The Intergenerational Literacy Project in which the families participate is one component of a partnership between the community and a local university. The program, which was in its sixth year at the time of the study, serves parents and other adult family members who wish to improve their own English literacy and language and who wish to become familiar with ways to support their children's education in U.S. schools.

Classes are offered in both the morning and evening. Parents who participate in day classes attend 4 days per week for 2 hours each day. Those who participate in evening classes attend 3 days per week for 2 hours each day. Classes are held in an adult-education setting located centrally within the community. Learners are grouped into multilingual, multilevel classes of 25 adults, and a flexible grouping model is used.

Each class is staffed by an instructional team of two literacy teachers and three literacy tutors per day. The teachers are graduate students at the university who are certified teachers with experience in literacy instruction, bilingual education, or adult education. Tutors include both federally funded College Work-Study students and community residents who were formerly learners in the program. Special effort is made to employ teachers and tutors who represent the languages and cultural backgrounds of families participating in the program.

As reported previously (Paratore, 1993, 1994), instruction in the Intergenerational Literacy Project classes was planned to achieve three goals: (1) provide opportunities for adults to read and respond to literacy materials of personal interest; (2) provide a selection of books, strategies, and ideas for adults to share with their children in order to support their literacy learning; and (3) provide a forum through which adults could share their family literacy experiences with their friends and teachers, enabling us all to learn more about the uses of literacy in diverse families. Heeding the cautions of researchers such as Auerbach (1989, 1995a, 1995b), emphasis is placed on situating literacy experiences within the fabric of daily life, rather than on the creation of school-like contexts in the home setting. Parents are encouraged to join with their children in multiple uses of literacy, including reading and writing oral histories, composing letters to friends and family members, journal keeping, and story writing and publishing. Parents also are taught how to help children with homework, the types of questions they might ask the classroom teacher to learn about their children's progress, and the types of questions they might ask their children to learn about the school day.

A typical class session consists of several instructional groupings. When they arrive, parents work individually to record their previous day's literacy activities and participate in discussion of literacy log entries. Next, the day's reading is presented, with teachers assessing and building on learners' previous knowledge of the topic, generating their predictions about the reading, and introducing key vocabulary. The article generally is displayed using an overhead projector and is either read aloud by a teacher, tutor, or learner, or is read chorally by the entire class. Following a brief discussion in which predictions are checked, learners divide into pairs or groups of three to five, each led by a teacher or tutor. In the small groups, participants reread the article closely, stopping frequently to discuss important ideas and vocabulary. After rereading, all members of the group, including teachers and tutors, respond in writing by summarizing, giving their opinions on what they read, or relating the reading to their own experiences. The class ends with parents and teachers sharing and discussing their responses to the reading. On at least a weekly basis, each class spends time in the program's computer lab where parents type and edit writing they have previously drafted and revised in class. Also, the program maintains a library of multilingual, multicultural children's books that parents are encouraged to take home to share with their children.

Although the common language of the classes is English and all class readings are in English, participants' first languages are integrated into instruction. In order to build on the wealth of knowledge learners bring to their developing English literacy, small groups often are conducted in parents' first languages and learners are encouraged to write in their chosen language.

During both morning and evening classes, free child care is provided for children of participating families, with preschool-aged children served in the morning and both preschool- and school-aged children attending in the evening. Twenty 3- and 4-year-old children are enrolled in an early childhood education classroom on site and participate in class while their parents study in the adult classrooms. Infants and toddlers of parents in the morning classes are provided with on-site child care led by a certified teacher and supported by a team of five child-care tutors per day. Infants, toddlers, and school-aged children are served in the evening child-care program. As in the morning, the child-care staff includes a certified teacher and a team of child-care tutors.

The child-care program is designed to facilitate children's language and literacy development. Using themed instructional units such as farm animals or methods of transportation, the program exposes children to a range of literature both in their first languages and in English. Frequent in-class storybook readings in both whole-class and small-group settings are supported by a variety of activities to meet the needs of all participating children. Activities offered include music, art, use of computers for story writing and instructional programs, and, with the school-aged children, homework support and a book discussion group.

Elementary school children attend one of four neighborhood schools in the community. Elementary teachers are familiar with the program and are notified of the children in their classrooms whose parents are participating. At the time that these data were collected, there was no other systematic interaction between the elementary and Intergenerational Literacy Project teachers.

Data from earlier studies (Paratore, 1993, 1994) indicate that adults who study within this instructional setting have higher rates of attendance and lower rates of attrition than do adults in traditional adult education programs. They also make more rapid gains in literacy achievement than those reported by adult learners in traditional settings, and they increase the practice of shared literacy with their preschool and school-aged children.

Participants

Twelve children were included in this study. They were chosen in the following way. First, we identified all the parents who entered the program after June 1994. Then, we identified parents in this group who had a child enrolled in Grades 2 through 5. We chose to begin with Grade 2 so that the child would have had 1 prior year of school experience for us to look back on. We chose to end with Grade 5 to avoid the confounding of evidence that might accompany the transition to middle school.

We contacted each parent in this subset of families and asked for permission to examine the home and school experiences of their children. We obtained permission from 17 parents. Five of the parents dropped out of the study prior to the end of the year.

Two pairs of children, Lucho and Luisa and Susana and Octavio, were siblings. At the time of the study, three of the subjects were in Grade 2, five were in Grade 3, two were in Grade 4, and two were in Grade 5. All the children spoke Spanish as a first language. Proficiency in English ranged from minimal to fluent. Their parents emigrated from several different countries: Colombia, the Dominican Republic, El Salvador, Guatemala, Honduras, and Puerto Rico. Eight children were placed in bilingual education classrooms and four were in general education classrooms. In three cases, children's schooling in the United States was interrupted by a return to their family's place of origin.

The children's parents joined the Intergenerational Literacy Project at different points during the academic year and, therefore, participated for varying lengths of time, ranging from 5 to 9 months. Of the 10 parents who participated, 7 were mothers and 3 were fathers. Parents' proficiency in English ranged from minimal to moderate. None of the parents was educated in the United States. Years of schooling in their places of origin ranged from 5 to 12 years. Years of residence in the United States ranged from 1 to 20 years. Table 1 summarizes the characteristics of the children and their families. On this table and throughout this book, pseudonyms are used to identify all study participants.

Data Collection

Several sources were used to answer the questions posed: (a) school history, including attendance records, report-card grades and comments, referrals for and placement in special services including Chapter 1 (an earlier name for Title I) and special education, and recommendations for and incidence of retention; (b) parent, teacher, and child interviews (audiotaped, transcribed, and translated as necessary); (c) intake interviews with parents upon entry to the literacy project; and (d) parents' self-report of family literacy practices.

Data From School History

We received written permission from parents and school officials to review all information in students' cumulative files. These provided records of attendance, report-card grades and comments, referrals for and placement in special services, and recommendations for and incidence of retention.

Data From Children's Teachers

Semistructured interviews were held with the teachers of both the present and the previous year. Interviewing questions and strategies were informed by Seidman (1991) and Mishler (1986). Interviews were characterized by open-ended questions intended to explore children's experiences with and development of literacy in the classroom and at home, and the teachers' impressions of the child's experiences and development and of the role the parents play in the

Table 1
Child and Parent Profiles

Child's name	Grade	Class type	Child's English proficiency	Child's years in U.S.	Parent enrolled in ILP	Parent's place of origin	Parent's years in U.S.	Parent's English proficiency	Parent's years in school	Months in ILP
Beatriz	2	General	Proficient	8	Father	El Salvador	13	Moderate	11	5
Jacinto	2	General	Moderate	7	Mother	Guatemala	7	Moderate	12	9
Lucho	2	Bilingual	Moderate	1.5	Father	Dominican Republic	5	Minimal	11	5
Ana	3	Bilingual	Moderate	6.5*	Mother	Puerto Rico	7*	Moderate	11	5
Belinda	3	Bilingual	Proficient	4	Mother	Honduras	4	Minimal	12 (Diploma)	9
Elena	3	General	Proficient	8	Father	Dominican Republic	20	Moderate	5	9
Juan	3	Bilingual	Moderate	3*	Mother	Colombia	3*	Minimal	10	5
Octavio	3	Bilingual	Minimal	1	Mother	Puerto Rico	1	Moderate	10	9
Luisa	4	Bilingual	Moderate	1.5	Father	Dominican Republic	5	Minimal	11	5
Susana	4	Bilingual	Moderate	1	Mother	Puerto Rico	1	Moderate	10	9
David	5	Bilingual	Moderate	3*	Mother	Puerto Rico	3*	Moderate	7	8
Benito	5	General	Proficient	10	Mother	Guatemala	12	Moderate	12 (Diploma)	5

* The period of residence in the United States was interrupted by a return to the family's place of origin.

child's school experiences. The questions presented in Appendix A provided a general outline for each interview, although after the opening prompt, researchers rarely followed the question format. Instead, as the conversation proceeded during each interview, the researcher reviewed the prompts to make certain that the discussion addressed each of the intended points.

The teacher from the previous year was interviewed once. Prior to the interview, the researcher reviewed information in the cumulative folder related to the previous year and obtained a copy of the previous year's report card. During the retrospective interview, the teacher was asked to review the report card and, at times, was reminded of an event recorded in the cumulative record to help prompt recall of the student's academic performance. The teacher with whom the child was placed at the time of the study was interviewed twice, once in the early spring and again at the end of the academic year.

All interviews were audiotaped, transcribed, and checked and corrected as necessary against the original audiotape by the researcher who conducted the interview.

Data From Parents

Data from parents were obtained through interviews, by reviewing the intake form completed when the parent entered the Intergenerational Literacy Project, and from the literacy logs the parent completed as part of the literacy class requirement. Parents were contacted by phone or in person to schedule the interviews. Interviews were conducted either in the parent's home or in one of the adult literacy classrooms. As with the teacher interview, interviews were semistructured. The prompts presented in Appendix B framed the content of the interviews, although the information generally was elicited during an informal conversation rather than by asking direct questions. Interview topics asked parents to comment on the ways children use literacy and language at home and on their general impressions of the child's school experiences.

Interviews were conducted in the informant's language of choice by a researcher who was fluent in the language. In all cases, parents chose to conduct the interview in Spanish. All interviews were audiotaped, transcribed, and checked and corrected as necessary against the original audiotape by the researcher who conducted the interview.

Transcriptions were translated by a member of the research team whose first language is Spanish.

Data from the intake forms (Appendix C) and literacy logs (Appendix D) were used to both augment and verify information gathered from parents, teachers, and children during the interviewing process. Intake forms were completed during an interview within 2 weeks of parents' enrollment in the literacy project. Literacy logs were completed by parents daily as part of the instructional routine in the project. The logs were two-sided forms. On one side parents were asked to record the literacy events they initiated to fulfill personal needs or goals; on the other side, parents were asked to record literacy events in which they engaged with their children. At the beginning of each instructional cycle, the project teachers introduced the literacy logs and explained the purpose to parents. Together, they discussed the types of episodes and events that parents might expect to record in their daily logs. During each week, parents often were invited to share and discuss entries in their logs with their teacher or with other learners.

Data From Parents' Teachers

Because the parents attended family literacy classes at the Intergenerational Literacy Project, their literacy teachers also provided a source of data. These teachers collected and submitted the parents' literacy logs and also related parents' comments about their children and their literacy interactions with them.

Data From Children

Children were interviewed once during the last quarter of the academic year. Interviews were scheduled by visiting the child's classroom teacher and arranging a convenient time to talk with the child. All interviews were conducted in school. Using the same open-ended, semistructured interview format described previously, children were asked to comment on their school experiences, the ways they use literacy at home, and their impressions of the ways their parents' participation in the Intergenerational Literacy Project has influenced family life. As in the other interviews, the prompts (presented in Appendix E) were used to focus the interviewer, but were not actually asked or used to sequence or restrict the conversation.

Interviews were conducted in the informant's language of choice by a researcher fluent in that language. Seven children chose to conduct the interview in English, and five chose to do so in Spanish. All interviews were audiotaped, transcribed, and checked and corrected as necessary against the original audiotape by the researcher who conducted the interview. Transcriptions were translated by a member of the research team whose first language is Spanish.

Data Analysis

A constant comparative method (Bogdan & Biklen, 1992; Strauss, 1987) of data collection and data analysis was used. Using inductive coding procedures described by Strauss and Corbin (1990), as interview data were collected, they were transcribed and, as necessary, translated. Transcripts and other data sources were reviewed line by line, labeled, and categorized. Researchers reviewed data and transcripts individually and collaboratively in research team meetings, coded and recoded, while searching for "key issues, recurrent events and activities" (Bogdan & Biklen, 1992, p. 74) across the multiple sources of data. As data were analyzed, they were used to raise issues that were explored in later interviews and to focus continued analyses of themes and incidents reported across all data sources. The qualitative research software, *HyperResearch*, was used to facilitate coding and analysis.

Twenty-one codes (presented in Appendix F) were identified early in the analysis process. These were eventually collapsed to form six categories of analysis: (1) language at home and at school, (2) literacy at home, (3) family's attention to school, (4) child's attitude toward school, (5) literacy at school, and (6) other performance indicators.

Following these analyses, two further types of analyses were conducted: within case and across case (Miles & Huberman, 1994). In within-case analyses, attention was paid to confirming a particular behavior or episode across multiple data sources. For example, if a parent mentioned specific types of family literacy interactions, we looked to see if the child and teacher provided evidence of similar types of events.

Data from the individual-case analyses were incorporated into a multiple-case and cross-case analysis. Cross-case analysis was conducted using a variable-oriented strategy (Miles & Huberman, 1994), as we looked for recurring themes and patterns across and within cases.

In reporting excerpts from the data, all literacy log entries are reported exactly as they were composed by the parent, with an accompanying English translation for entries that were composed in Spanish. In cases in which interviews were conducted in Spanish, they were transcribed and then translated. In this report, we have chosen to present interview data in the language in which the informant provided it to us and, when appropriate, to provide an English translation. On occasion, we have edited remarks to conform to standard Spanish. In those cases, we have identified edited segments by placing them in brackets.

Our review of the individual case studies suggests that, although the uniqueness of the circumstances and experiences of each of the children were of critical importance in understanding their success or their struggle, the commonalities among their experiences were equally instructive. Therefore, the cross-case analysis, in which we sought to determine the ways in which the children's home and school experiences were similar or different and to what extent such experiences might suggest eventual success or failure in school, provides the foundation for the presentation of cases in the chapters that follow. In accordance with our data analyses, the cases are organized within three categories: cases in which children were highly successful in school, cases in which children were experiencing moderate success and were seemingly "on their way" to high achievement, and cases in which children were struggling in school.

CHAPTER 3

Children Who Were Highly Successful in School

In this chapter we discuss the home and school literacy and language experiences of three students, Beatriz, Belinda, and Elena, all of whom were consistently high performers in school. Beatriz was an 8-year-old child who attended a general education second-grade classroom in a public school. She lived with her mother and father, who were from El Salvador, and she was the youngest of three children. Belinda was a 9-year-old girl who was enrolled in a bilingual third-grade class. She was born in Honduras and had lived in the United States with her family for nearly 5 years and in this community for 4 years. She lived with her parents and her 1-year-old brother Carlitos. Elena was an 8-year-old child attending a general education third-grade classroom. Her parents emigrated from the Dominican Republic 20 years before the study. She lived with her mother, father, and older sister.

In two cases (Beatriz and Elena), the child's father was the participant in the Intergenerational Literacy Project, and in one case (Belinda), the child's mother was the participant. Parents had resided in the United States for a wide range of years (4 to 20). Two parents had completed 11 or 12 years of schooling in their own countries and were able to read in Spanish. One parent, Elena's father, Miguel, had completed 5 years of schooling in his country and had not learned to read or write in Spanish. In the ILP, he was learning to read in English. The parents described their English proficiency as either minimal or moderate.

Language at Home and at School

Two of the children, Beatriz and Elena, had been in general education classrooms since first enrolling in school. They were each described by parents and teachers as being fully bilingual, speaking English in school and primarily Spanish at home. For example, Alfredo, Beatriz's father, assessed his daughter's language proficiency in the following way:

Beatriz sabe hablar en los dos idiomas. Beatriz es bilingüe. Sí, ella sabe hablar, leer y escribir en inglés y en español. Claro, naturalmente ella sabe más inglés porque es el idioma que ella más está practicando.	*Beatriz knows how to speak both languages. Beatriz is bilingual. She knows how to speak, read, and write in English and in Spanish. Naturally, she knows more English because it is the language she uses more.*

Elena's father reported that "we constantly use Spanish in the house." During several literacy project family events, Miguel's literacy teacher observed him and his daughters speaking Spanish together. Elena, however, noted that she often chose to speak English at home for her father's benefit:

Because I want him to learn some words and I'll speak in English. Like some words I haven't heard in English. I want him to learn them while I am talking English.

At school, Elena's primary language was English, and her teachers reported never hearing her speak Spanish.

The third student, Belinda, was reported to use both English and Spanish in school and primarily Spanish at home. She was in a bilingual education classroom and had been since her enrollment in school. According to her teacher, Mr. Vásquez, English was increasingly emphasized because he was preparing Belinda, and most of the other students in the class, to be mainstreamed into an English-only classroom the following year. Mr. Vásquez reported that Belinda's English proficiency had improved over the course of the year, while her Spanish had remained at the same level. He said that although at the beginning of the school year she spoke almost entirely in Spanish in the classroom, at the end of the year she chose to use English most of the time and her English proficiency was excellent.

Mr. Vásquez commented that Belinda's parents supported his efforts to increase her use of English:

> I was talking to her mother during a PTO the last time I saw her. She was, she told me, "I don't mind if you tell her to speak only in English, that's what I want." So I think, you know, it's both in the classroom and at home that we've encouraged her to speak more English than Spanish.

Later in the interview, he returned to this topic:

> They don't mind if she forgets the Spanish. You know, they want it, yes, because it's part of their culture, but the main focus is English and they know, they understand, you know, they, I think they'll do anything just to have her ready.

The data suggested to us that in these three families, parents and children had what we came to call a "balanced" attitude toward language learning and use: In each case, parents expressed an interest and desire in having children acquire and maintain proficiency in Spanish language and literacy, but they also emphasized the importance of proficiency in English language and literacy. In all cases, children and their parents used Spanish at home in the course of routine conversations and dialogue. When engaged in particular literacy and language activities, they purposefully chose English to extend English language and literacy of either the parent or the child, or both.

Literacy at Home

The three children and their parents were routinely involved in the practice of family literacy, reporting that they frequently engaged in storybook reading together and alone. In Elena's case, for example, her father Miguel's literacy log and comments to his literacy teachers indicated that he read books from the project library at home and that he shared them with Elena:

> Last night I ris [read] to my dautas [daughters] the new year [*The New Year*]. Elena she like [liked] the histor [story]. [literacy log, 1/25/95]

In response to questions about reading at home, Elena also said,

> I always get a book and I tell my father, "Do you want to read it with me?" and sometimes he does and sometimes he doesn't.

Elena also reported reading by herself:

Interviewer: Can you tell me about reading at home?

Elena: In second grade, my teacher gave everybody for Christmas a book and we, and I always read that book. I never forget it.

Interviewer: What was the book?

Elena: *Ready, Get Set, Read.*

Interviewer: Uh huh.

Elena: And I always read that book. My favorite story is, um, riddles and that's, I like the riddles and this is on it and my favorite story is *Papa Bear and the Three Goldilocks* too. And the *Three Little Bears* and *Little Red Riding Hood.* That's my favorite one.

During Beatriz's interview, she reported that storybook reading was a routine activity at home: "Mostly everyday...I read a book in my house." In response to the interviewer's questions, she elaborated:

Interviewer: What kinds of books do you read at home? Where do you get them?

Beatriz: Some at the store and the other ones I get at the library because I have a library card.

Interviewer: So do you sometimes go to the library after school to get the books?

Beatriz: Yeah.

Interviewer: What book are you reading now at home?

Beatriz: Um, right now, I am not reading none of them because I just finished one and I gotta pick one today that I am gonna read.

Interviewer: Oh, OK. So what are you going to do today after school?

Beatriz: Pick a book and read it.

Interviewer: At the library?

Beatriz: Yeah.

Storybook reading at home allowed many opportunities for intergenerational learning, as her father Alfredo said,

A veces ella quiere…que leamos juntos, que leamos una parte cada uno…. Le encanta leer conmigo porque me dice, "bueno voy a leer yo, después lee Ud." Y así leemos un capítulo…entonces el inglés a veces yo no entiendo muy bien, también. Entonces ella me los explica. Como ella aprende mucho inglés en la escuela entonces ella sabe mucho…yo me quedo corto en el inglés con ella…. Me dice "Papi esto quiere decir esto, y esto esto." Me lo explica en español. "Y pasa esto porque en la historia tal, sucede esto y esto con los personajes." Ella me lo explica así en detalle.

Sometimes she wants us to read together, that each one reads one part…. She loves to read with me because she tells me, "Well I'll read and then you read." And like that, we read one chapter... then the English—sometimes I don't understand well. So she explains it to me. Since she learns a lot of English at school. So she knows a lot...I am no match for her in English. She says, "Daddy, this means this and this this." She explains it to me in Spanish, "and this happens because in the story, this happens and this with the characters." She explains it to me with lots of detail.

Beatriz also explained that sharing books together was a new family event. After she mentioned that she and her father read together at home, the interviewer asked the following:

Interviewer: That is different? Did he read to you before?

Beatriz: No 'cause he didn't go to school before and now that he brings the books he reads the books too.

In Belinda's case, the practice of reading at home was longstanding. Upon entry to the literacy program, for example, her mother Gloria reported that she shared stories or read with her children daily in both English and Spanish. She also noted that she took her daughter to the public library twice a month. Her literacy log entries reflected routine storybook reading, with *La gallinita roja* (*The Little Red Hen*) a favorite in both Spanish and English:

Yesterday I read the book my daughter was very happy because she like read the Hen red book. [literacy log, 11/29/94]

Yesterday in the afternoon I read a [to] my daughter but no entendí algunas palabras (*but I didn't understand some words*) [literacy log, 1/19/95]

Yesterday I helped my daughter read a book in Spanish. [literacy log, 2/6/95]

Yesterday my daughter came with me to school. She read La gallinita Roja for the other children. The children liked the story she read. [literacy log, 2/23/95]

This morning before I came to the Enghlis [sic] class I read *The Ugly Duckling* to my daughter and after she came with me to school. [literacy log, 4/15/95]

However, Gloria noted that her participation in the Intergenerational Literacy Project had increased the ways she and Belinda shared literacy.

Antes, no tenía la curiosidad de coger un libro, un diccionario y buscar tal palabra. Ahora lo hago más seguido. También he notado que leo mejor y entiendo más lo que leo. Otra cosa es que entiendo que mientras más aprendo es mejor para mí, para mi futuro. De esta manera, podré ayudarle más al pequeño que tengo y tal vez no pase las dificultades que he pasado con la niña.

Before I did not have the curiosity to pick up a book, a dictionary to look up a word. Now I do it more often. I have also noticed that I read better and understand better. I am also aware that the more I learn the better it is for my future. This way I will be able to help the little one more and maybe won't have the difficulties that I have had with the girl.

In addition to daily reading, all three children engaged in frequent writing activities for numerous reasons. They reported writing letters to friends and family members and notes to one another in order to accomplish routine tasks in the course of the day. Most notable was that all children reported writing stories for themselves or to share with others. Beatriz, for example, said she wrote "stories by myself at my house" which she later shared with her brothers and parents. Belinda said, "I write stories at home when we are on vacation and...when I come...when I'm home, I sometimes write what happen[ed] to me at school."

In Elena's case, there was rich information about writing, suggesting she carried strategies she learned in school into her uses of literacy at home: "When I'm done reading sometimes I like to write what happened in the story, the beginning, the middle, and the end."

In each of these families, parents and children were explicitly aware that they were learning together, that their literacy interactions were benefiting both parent and child. Comments from Elena and her father, Miguel, are representative. Elena noted, "My father always sees me write and sometimes he gets a paper and draws some of the pictures and things and he writes and while I am drawing. Sometimes he reads those stories by himself so he could concentrate."

Miguel reported in his literacy log:

> My daughter help[s] me a lot I feel happy because my daughter help[s me with] writing. [literacy log, 3/28/95]

Elena reported that she spoke English to her father "because I want to help him to learn some words." When asked about her Spanish reading, she suggested that her father helps her: "When I don't know a word, I ask José [a relative] or my father and they tell me and then my father tries to practice it in English. I remember the word and he practices."

Gloria noted that she and Belinda increasingly supported each other's learning:

Yo noto que ahora puedo ayudarla más con sus tareas, quizás con algunas palabras que ella no sepa y yo sí. Siento que puedo ayudarla más porque me siento bien segura.... Ella me ayuda cuando tal vez yo sé escribir una palabra pero no sé pronunciarla, ella me ayuda en eso. También me ayuda cuando estamos viendo algún programa, ella me dice lo que hablan y de qué se trata. Ella está aprendiendo a escribir el inglés ahora pero habla bastante.

I have noticed that now I can help her more with her homework. Sometimes with words she doesn't understand and I do. I feel I can help her more because I feel more confident.... She helps me when I know how to spell a word but can't pronounce it, she helps me with pronunciation. She also helps me when we are watching TV; she tells me what the people are saying and what the program is about. She is learning to write English now, but she speaks a lot.

The same theme was evident in Alfredo's responses:

| Ella digamos…cuando estamos en casa siempre me está platicando de la escuela mía, y yo también le platico [sobre lo] que estoy aprendiendo…. Por ejemplo, ayer fuimos a la librería [biblioteca] y ella estaba fascinada porque a mí me habían dado un library card porque ella la tenía hace tiempo… desde cuando ella comenzó el primer grado ella tuvo library card…. Entonces ella me dice: "¡Papi!" Y ella sale a dar la noticia con los dos hermanos y a toda la familia de que yo tengo una library card también. | *Let's see…when we are home, she is always chatting about my school, and I chat with her as well, about what I am learning…. For example, yesterday we went to the library, and she was fascinated that I had a library card, because she has had it for a long time...since she started first grade…. Then she tells me, "Daddy!" And she ran out to give the news to her two siblings and to the whole family that I also have a library card.* |

Alfredo returned to this topic again later in the interview:

| Cuando ella sabe que yo voy a la escuela ella siempre me pregunta, se interesa por saber: "Papi, ¿qué hizo ahora en la escuela?" Ella siempre me pregunta: "Papi, ¿va a ir a la escuela?" me dice también… un día antes, "si va a la escuela por favor me trae un libro." Como ella sabe de que yo llevo libros de aquí…. Ella está muy interesada. Entonces, pues a ella, a ella le gusta cuando sabe que yo estoy haciendo algo, especialmente que le interesa a ella también. | *When she knows that I'm going to school, she always asks me, she is interested in knowing: "Daddy, what did you do at school?" She always asks me, "Daddy, are you going to school?" She also tells me…a day before, "If you go to school, please bring me a book," because she knows that I take books home from here…. She is very interested. So then, well, she likes it when she knows that I'm doing something, especially something that also interests her.* |

Family's Attention to School

In addition to reading, writing, and talking together, in each of these families, parents were highly and consistently attentive to children's formal schooling. They checked their children's homework daily and helped with its completion when necessary. In Beatriz's case, both parents had frequent contact with her teachers. They inquired when they had particular questions about a report-card grade or comment, about homework assignments, or about Beatriz's behavior. Beatriz's first-grade teacher, for instance, commented,

> The mother…she would pick her up at the end of the day, but she was quiet and more shy than the father [who]…was very involved. He came in the classroom every opportunity we extended to have parents come in. He readily volunteered and participated and we did two parent workshops which he attended and he was delightful. I mean he's so supportive of everything we did in the classroom and I think the mother also was supportive of academics and the children doing well in school but she didn't feel as comfortable coming in and conversing with us as he did but…they were supportive of everything she did…took her to the library, got her books, did everything to support her and she did well as a result of it.

In addition to her parents, Beatriz's older siblings also paid attention to her school activities. As described by her first-grade teacher, Mrs. Margolis, Beatriz's schooling was a family affair:

> They were reading at home with her and they were taking her to the library, the older children were taking her to the library and the family, and even the older daughter came in and read to the class when we extended the invitation…so they were supportive of her learning to read and making it exciting.

Alfredo was proud of the support he and other family members provided Beatriz in school and attributed his daughter's success in school to what they did at home: "tal vez también porque nosotros se lo enseñamos bien en casa" (*"perhaps also because we teach her things quite well at home"*). He also explained that despite not having much free time, he tried to find time to help his children, especially Beatriz, because she was the youngest and thus "in the process of learning":

Claro que no me queda mucho
tiempo a veces porque también
trabajo y tengo muchas otras activi-
dades…para atenderlos a ellos…
entonces no me queda demasiado
tiempo libre, pero el poquito tiempo
que a veces me queda, yo se lo
dedico, más que todo a ella porque
como está pequeña, está en proceso

*Of course I don't have much
free time because I also work
and have many other activities…
to help them…so I don't have
much free time but the little
time I sometimes have I
dedicate it, mostly to her for she
is the youngest, she is in the
process of learning and I try to*

de aprendizaje y, este, yo le trato de   *help her the most I can.*
ayudar lo más que puedo.

On the other hand, Belinda's parents attended formal school functions and responded to the teachers' notes, but seldom initiated contact with her teachers. Belinda's teacher in both second and third grades, Mr. Vásquez, noted that the family environment seemed to support her strong participation in the classroom and that "her parents are very supportive." He also commented on the intergenerational nature of the learning that occurred at home:

> A few days ago, she [Belinda] was telling me about her mother being in school and that she tries to help her mommy…. [she said] "I try to help her because I know a little bit of English."

Mr. Vásquez noted that Belinda's mother attended formal school functions, such as Parent Teacher Organization (PTO) meetings, and responded to notes from him requesting that she visit, but that she did not otherwise visit the school. He reported that he routinely asked parents to read and write with their children at home and asked the parents to sign a paper stating what the child read and wrote. Gloria, Belinda's mother, explained that when she received these requests she felt comfortable providing her own assessment of Belinda's performance:

> Creo que cuando los niños tienen muchas vacaciones, cuando regresan a la escuela, se les olvida muchas cosas, la lectura más que todo. Ella no estaba leyendo muy corrido. El maestro mandó una carta y mi comentario fue que yo noté que la niña estaba leyendo más despacio.
>
> *I believe that when students go on long vacations, when they return to school they forget many things, especially reading. She was not reading very fluently. The teacher sent me a letter and my comment was that my child was reading slower.*

Gloria kept herself informed about the subjects her daughter studied and the ways in which English and Spanish were used in her classroom, routinely asking her about her day at school and helping her with her homework. During her interview, Gloria commented on the ways she helped Belinda with her homework:

> Ayudarle en sus tareas, sobre todo de matemática. Cuando ella me lee,
>
> *I help her with her homework, especially math. When she reads*

me gusta hacerle preguntas sobre lo que ha entendido de la lectura. Le ayudo a analizar las lecturas que le dejan de tarea.	*to me, I like to ask her questions about what she understands from the reading. I help her analyze her reading homework.*

Gloria's literacy log entries also provide evidence of the support she provided Belinda:

Ayer puse [estuve] enseñandole [enseñándole a] mi hija a ser [hacer] una tarea que tenia [tenía] de mate- maticas [matemáticas].	*Yesterday I was teaching my daughter to do her mathematics homework.* [literacy log, 11/2/94]

Yesterday my daughter have [sic] homework the mathematics and sci- ence. I helped her with homework, after she watch [sic] TV with me. [lit- eracy log, 11/30/94]

This morning I helped my daughter check her mathematics homework but I did not find errors. [literacy log, 3/14/95]

When I help my daugther [sic] with her homework she is very happy and I also learn to read and write. [literacy log, 6/14/95]

Elena's parents, too, seldom went to school and may have been discouraged from attending or initiating meetings because of their limited English proficiency. Elena's teacher recalled a parent confer- ence early in the year when Elena's mother was very attentive, but seemed to understand little of what she said. Despite the lack of teacher interaction and classroom visits, Miguel and his wife paid at- tention to Elena's education in other ways. Miguel reported on his literacy project intake form (see Appendix C) that he asked his chil- dren about their homework on a daily basis. He confirmed this dur- ing his interview the following spring:

Les chequeo algunas veces las tareas de ellas a ver cómo se están comportando en la escuela y están haciendo muy bien...cuando no las ayudo yo, las ayuda mi esposa.	*I check their [his daughters'] homework sometimes to see how they are behaving in school and they are doing very good work... when I don't help them, my wife does.*

Miguel's interest in his daughters' schoolwork was confirmed by his literacy teacher, who reported that Miguel brought samples of their work to class and discussed their grades with her.

Child's Attitude Toward School

With regard to motivation and interest in learning, these three children had very similar profiles. They each reported that they enjoyed school and learning and they all were described by teachers and parents as being highly motivated by and interested in schooling.

During her interview, Belinda stated that she enjoyed each of her classes and her positive attitude was confirmed in conversations with both her teacher and her mother. Mr. Vásquez reported that Belinda frequently told him that she was having fun at school. Gloria credited Mr. Vásquez for Belinda's interest in school: "A ella le gusta que el maestro le diga que ella puede hacer algo porque ella siente que puede" (*"She likes it that her teacher tells her that she can do something because then she feels that she can"*).

Similarly, Beatriz was portrayed as a dedicated and achieving student who was always among the top students in her classes. Her father said, "Es muy aplicada...y tiene mucha energía en la escuela" (*"She applies herself...and has a lot of energy in school"*). Her previous and present teachers described her as interested and involved in all classroom activities. For example, Mrs. Margolis, her first-grade teacher said, "She was an excellent student...a wonderful student, she did everything you'd ever ask her to do. I don't think she ever misbehaved. She was just a delight, an absolute delight."

Throughout his interview, Alfredo said that he knew his daughter was good at school. He said that he had always received compliments from her teachers and also noted that "los homeworks son demasiado fáciles para ella" (*"homework is too easy for her"*). Her father saw her as "una muchachita muy precoz, sí, muy inteligente" (*"a very precocious little girl, yes, very intelligent"*). These comments were consistent with the grades Beatriz received on her report cards, on which there was evidence of excellent achievement and progress.

Elena's second- and third-grade teachers also described her as a motivated and cooperative child who was interested and involved in classroom activities. Elena's second-grade teacher, for example, recalled that she "had a very good effort" and was "nice to the group." She also commented that Elena was "easy to work with." She described Elena as "receptive [to] any type of instruction that you would give her. She wasn't resistant at all. She wanted to learn and knew that we wanted to help her."

Her third-grade teacher, Mrs. Martin, was new to the school, having replaced a teacher just 8 weeks earlier. Her description of Elena's attitude and behaviors was similar to that of the second-grade teacher. She said that Elena was "quite enthusiastic. I very rarely see her when she's not ready to cooperate, ready to learn, or ready to participate in any of the activities of a typical classroom." Elena's self-report was consistent with her teachers' observations. She stated that she liked school a lot and enjoyed all of her school subjects.

All three children were also students who had excellent school attendance. Belinda had only three absences (98%) in the second grade, and she earned an attendance award, having had only one absence (99%) in the third grade. Beatriz's school attendance during both first (93%) and second (94%) grades was equally and consistently high. Similarly, Elena missed a total of 6 school days in second and third grade, achieving attendance rates of 96% and 99% in each of the 2 years.

Literacy at School

In each of these cases, during the 2 years in which data were collected, the children were enrolled in classrooms where teachers were recognized by administrators and colleagues as being particularly effective. In their own reports, teachers described programs that offered children extensive opportunities to practice reading and writing throughout the school day. Field notes recorded by researchers during the periods when they interviewed teachers in their classrooms documented learning environments that were rich in books and other types of print and where the products of literacy activities and events were displayed prominently.

Mr. Vásquez, Belinda's teacher in both second and third grades, described his literacy program as one that incorporated small-group and paired work and routine parent-child reading and writing at home:

Mr. Vásquez: Well, on a typical day she'll participate in, first in reading. We'll be in cooperative groups, and in cooperative groups what we do, they read with partners, they also do read-alouds, and they read to their groups, group, individual, group.... Sometimes, you know, I moved the students around so there's some kind of variation, but, you know, most of the time, the members stay the same so they can get used to each other.

Interviewer: And what about writing?

Mr. Vásquez: Writing is almost the same process. It'll be in cooperative groups again. There's a lot of individual writing, independent writing. Homework, it's, most of the time is writing and there at houses, at home with their parents sometimes and, um, I just forgot the reading also is with their parents. I assign reading assignments. Sometimes they read books, short books, to their parents and the parents have to sign a paper stating that the child read to me such and such a page, so the writing, too.

Elena's third-grade classroom was taught by Mrs. Martin, a monolingual English speaker. During the daily 1-hour literacy instruction block, Mrs. Martin was joined by a Chapter 1 coteacher, also a monolingual English speaker. Mrs. Martin reported that the classroom literacy routines included daily journal writing, keeping reading logs, and sustained silent reading. In direct reading instruction, she noted emphasizing a variety of strategies: "In her reading program at school using the basal reader, we discuss predictions and background-building experiences, vocabulary, and reader's response questions to the story that we read in class as a group."

During both first and second grades, Beatriz's teachers, too, provided a variety of literacy activities infused throughout the school day, incorporating opportunities to read and write individually, in pairs, in small groups, and with the entire class.

In school, each of the children was judged to be a highly successful student. Beatriz was described by her first-grade teacher as "a wonderful reader and a wonderful writer." Ms. Margolis said the following:

From the initial start she just took off with reading. She loved it. She couldn't wait to learn and, as soon as she learned, she was the ideal student because you didn't have to encourage her to practice—she was practicing all the time on her own, so she just kept getting better and better.

Her second-grade teacher, Ms. Kavanagh, reported that Beatriz continued to do very well and was at the top of her class. Her motivation and interest in literacy activities at school were corroborated by her father, who pointed out that among her favorite school activities were drawing and especially reading:

A ella le gusta mucho dibujar…y además de eso lo que a ella sí le encanta mucho también es la lectura. Ella lee, lee y lee…pero en la lectura ella es fenomenal…. Ella se lee libros, ella devora libro tras libro, leyendo. A ella le encanta leer.	*She likes very much to draw… aside from that what she is really enchanted by is reading. She reads, reads and reads…but in reading she is phenomenal…. She reads books, she devours book after book, reading them. She loves reading.*

In describing the types of books Beatriz read, her father also gave us an indication of the teachers' influence on the type of reading she did at home:

Ahora lo que ella lee son chapter books que le recomiendan en la escuela, porque la maestra misma que tiene ahora allá en la escuela, ella le dice de que Beatriz ya debe de leer chapter books fuertes porque Beatriz es muy avanzada.	*Now, what she reads now are chapter books that they recommend at school because the teacher she has now, she tells her that she should start reading difficult books, chapter books because Beatriz is very advanced.*

Beatriz confirmed what her teachers and her father said about her interest in reading at school. She identified DEAR time ("Drop Everything and Read") as her favorite part of the school day and added, "My sister says that I'm a bookworm. I love books." Beatriz reported reading two books at the same time, one at home and one at school:

Interviewer: What books are you reading now?

Beatriz: The one in school?

Interviewer: Mhmm.

Beatriz: This one.

Table 2
Children Who Were Successful in School

Child's name	Language at home	Language at school	English proficiency	Literacy at home	Family's attention to school	Literacy at school	English literacy	Spanish literacy	Attitude toward school	Attendance
Beatriz	Spanish and English	English	Fluent	Daily shared and self-initiated reading and writing	Frequently visited school; monitored homework daily	Highly systematic with daily opportunities for extended reading and writing	Above grade level	Above grade level	Excellent attitude and behavior	94%
Belinda	Spanish	Primarily English; some Spanish	Fluent	Daily shared and self-initiated reading and writing	Attended formal school events; monitored homework daily	Highly systematic with daily opportunities for extended reading and writing	On grade level	On grade level	Excellent attitude and behavior	99%
Elena	Spanish and English	English	Fluent	Daily shared and self-initiated reading and writing	Rarely attended school events; monitored homework daily	Highly systematic with daily opportunities for extended reading and writing	On grade level	Unknown	Excellent attitude and behavior	99%

Interviewer: This one. Beverly Cleary, *Beezus and Ramona*. So you like the time when you get to read by yourself the best?

Beatriz: Yeah.

Interviewer: What is it that you like about books?

Beatriz: That sometimes…there are fairy tales and I like the fantasy they have. This one—it's not really true but it has things that can really happen because this is just a story. And I like the characters in the story too.

In commenting on her interest in writing, Beatriz said, "It's fun, I like it too, but sometimes I am a little bit messy." When asked what type of writing activities she does at school, she explained,

> We used to write summaries of stories and now we write…math. We write about the things we say on the rug sometimes. We write them down on the paper too. And…in reading groups…we have to make another…summary about that story…the characters, setting, problem, and solution of the story.

Beatriz's interest and high achievement in literacy was confirmed in all sources of data. Her report card grades over the 2-year period were exceptional. They were either Ys (yes, displays skill consistently) or Ps (is making steady progress).

Belinda, similarly, was described by her teacher as being "among the highest in the class in both English and Spanish reading." He said, "Can I give you a scale of 1 to 10? She's around 8, um, 9." He explained that she is "an enthusiastic reader [who] chooses to read on her own" after she had finished an assignment before other students or during recess. He noted that her greatest weakness in reading was her pronunciation in English. Both she and her teacher reported that she chose to read in both Spanish and English in school. In terms of writing, he reported that he had observed substantial growth between second grade and late in third grade because she was writing more creatively.

Belinda's report-card grades during both years of the study were consistently "satisfactory." In second grade, she received Bs (on an A–F scale) in reading, writing, language (Spanish), English as a Second Language, and spelling. In third grade, she received all S's (for "Consistently Progressing") and Ps (for "Progressing") in written language, speaking and listening, and reading. She received all S's for conduct and work habits.

Elena's experiences differed from those of Beatriz and Belinda. She struggled in reading in second grade and participated in the school's Chapter 1 program. At the end of second grade, her teachers reported that she was making good progress, but that she continued to experience difficulty, particularly in decoding. During the interview with Elena's second-grade teachers, they recalled that she required help with grade-level reading and writing tasks. They remembered that she struggled when reading new words and often needed prompts to help her decode successfully. Portfolio evaluations that were included in her permanent record confirmed these recollections. Elena was consistently evaluated as "needing some help" to accomplish grade-level tasks. Her second-grade teachers also remembered that during independent reading time she often did not choose books that she could read successfully. On her report card, she was assigned a 3 in language arts on a scale of 1–4 in which 1 indicated "highly skilled" and 4 indicated "lacking important skills." On the placement form at the end of second grade, her teachers wrote, "Elena has made good progress in reading this year. However, she still needs support in order to continue her growth. She is recommended for Chapter 1 services next year."

By the middle of third grade, Elena appeared to be making fine progress in reading and writing. Her teacher, Mrs. Martin, observed that Elena "has a strong vocabulary, a strong sense of comprehension, and I have yet to determine what her weaknesses might be. I've only been in the classroom 6 weeks. Actually 7 weeks."

At the end of third grade, Mrs. Martin commented that Elena was "quite verbal" and "very able to express herself," shows "strong vocabulary and strong comprehension" with "no evident weaknesses." She seemed to perceive Elena as an average student: "She's not a top student, I wouldn't say, but she's right in the middle."

Mrs. Martin observed that Elena was very interested in reading, and said that she was "quite often sitting there with a book," and added,

> She's one of the first people in the morning to arrive every day. And, she usually does go right to it, see and pick up a book or take up her writing journal and begins either, either choice in the morning.

Elena's records from the Chapter 1 program indicated that on performance assessment task completed with her Chapter 1 teacher near the end of third grade, Elena required some support from the teacher to achieve the grade-level standard. The teacher did note, however, that she had made "substantial growth" over the course of the third-grade year, and on a scale from 1 to 3, in which 1 indicated minimal growth and 3 indicated substantial growth, Elena received a rank of 3.

Miguel's perception of his daughter Elena's school literacy performance differed from her second-grade teachers' description of her literacy skills (Elena's Chapter 1 reading teacher and her classroom teacher), and her third-grade teacher's assessment. During his interview and in conversations with his literacy teacher about Elena's schoolwork, Miguel never indicated that he was aware that Elena participated in a remedial reading program. Commenting on both his daughters' school performances, he said, "They are doing very good work and I feel happy in that aspect...they are doing well, getting very good grades, both of them."

Miguel was aware of and pleased about some of the special opportunities his daughter had to learn literacy in school. He seemed to perceive this both as a help to her and also as evidence of her success:

La niña mía les lee libros a los más pequeños en el kindergarten...la maestra de ella la pone a leerles libros a los niños más pequeños, y yo veo que es una gran cosa porque veo que está más sobresaliente en todo a ella siempre la están buscando [para que participe] en actividades, bien activa ella, la más chica.	*My girl [Elena] reads books to the smallest children in the kindergarten...her teacher has her read books to the smallest children, and I see that this is a great thing because I see that she is more outstanding in everything because they are always looking for her to participate in activities she's very active, the little one.*

A review of Elena's report cards suggested diminished academic performance between Grades 2 and 3. Her report-card grades dropped from mostly Bs in Grade 2 to mostly Cs in Grade 3. However, comments from her teachers during interviews suggested that her academic performance was strengthening, rather than weakening, and that the differences in her grades were due to different grading standards adhered to by teachers from year to year.

Interviewer: This one. Beverly Cleary, *Beezus and Ramona*. So you like the time when you get to read by yourself the best?

Beatriz: Yeah.

Interviewer: What is it that you like about books?

Beatriz: That sometimes…there are fairy tales and I like the fantasy they have. This one—it's not really true but it has things that can really happen because this is just a story. And I like the characters in the story too.

In commenting on her interest in writing, Beatriz said, "It's fun, I like it too, but sometimes I am a little bit messy." When asked what type of writing activities she does at school, she explained,

We used to write summaries of stories and now we write...math. We write about the things we say on the rug sometimes. We write them down on the paper too. And…in reading groups…we have to make another…summary about that story…the characters, setting, problem, and solution of the story.

Beatriz's interest and high achievement in literacy was confirmed in all sources of data. Her report card grades over the 2-year period were exceptional. They were either Ys (yes, displays skill consistently) or Ps (is making steady progress).

Belinda, similarly, was described by her teacher as being "among the highest in the class in both English and Spanish reading." He said, "Can I give you a scale of 1 to 10? She's around 8, um, 9." He explained that she is "an enthusiastic reader [who] chooses to read on her own" after she had finished an assignment before other students or during recess. He noted that her greatest weakness in reading was her pronunciation in English. Both she and her teacher reported that she chose to read in both Spanish and English in school. In terms of writing, he reported that he had observed substantial growth between second grade and late in third grade because she was writing more creatively.

Belinda's report-card grades during both years of the study were consistently "satisfactory." In second grade, she received Bs (on an A–F scale) in reading, writing, language (Spanish), English as a Second Language, and spelling. In third grade, she received all S's (for "Consistently Progressing") and Ps (for "Progressing") in written language, speaking and listening, and reading. She received all S's for conduct and work habits.

Elena's experiences differed from those of Beatriz and Belinda. She struggled in reading in second grade and participated in the school's Chapter 1 program. At the end of second grade, her teachers reported that she was making good progress, but that she continued to experience difficulty, particularly in decoding. During the interview with Elena's second-grade teachers, they recalled that she required help with grade-level reading and writing tasks. They remembered that she struggled when reading new words and often needed prompts to help her decode successfully. Portfolio evaluations that were included in her permanent record confirmed these recollections. Elena was consistently evaluated as "needing some help" to accomplish grade-level tasks. Her second-grade teachers also remembered that during independent reading time she often did not choose books that she could read successfully. On her report card, she was assigned a 3 in language arts on a scale of 1–4 in which 1 indicated "highly skilled" and 4 indicated "lacking important skills." On the placement form at the end of second grade, her teachers wrote, "Elena has made good progress in reading this year. However, she still needs support in order to continue her growth. She is recommended for Chapter 1 services next year."

By the middle of third grade, Elena appeared to be making fine progress in reading and writing. Her teacher, Mrs. Martin, observed that Elena "has a strong vocabulary, a strong sense of comprehension, and I have yet to determine what her weaknesses might be. I've only been in the classroom 6 weeks. Actually 7 weeks."

At the end of third grade, Mrs. Martin commented that Elena was "quite verbal" and "very able to express herself," shows "strong vocabulary and strong comprehension" with "no evident weaknesses." She seemed to perceive Elena as an average student: "She's not a top student, I wouldn't say, but she's right in the middle."

Mrs. Martin observed that Elena was very interested in reading, and said that she was "quite often sitting there with a book," and added,

> She's one of the first people in the morning to arrive every day. And, she usually does go right to it, see and pick up a book or take up her writing journal and begins either, either choice in the morning.

Elena's records from the Chapter 1 program indicated that on a performance assessment task completed with her Chapter 1 teacher near the end of third grade, Elena required some support from the teacher to achieve the grade-level standard. The teacher did note, however, that she had made "substantial growth" over the course of the third-grade year, and on a scale from 1 to 3, in which 1 indicated minimal growth and 3 indicated substantial growth, Elena received a rank of 3.

Miguel's perception of his daughter Elena's school literacy performance differed from her second-grade teachers' description of her literacy skills (Elena's Chapter 1 reading teacher and her classroom teacher), and her third-grade teacher's assessment. During his interview and in conversations with his literacy teacher about Elena's schoolwork, Miguel never indicated that he was aware that Elena participated in a remedial reading program. Commenting on both his daughters' school performances, he said, "They are doing very good work and I feel happy in that aspect...they are doing well, getting very good grades, both of them."

Miguel was aware of and pleased about some of the special opportunities his daughter had to learn literacy in school. He seemed to perceive this both as a help to her and also as evidence of her success:

La niña mía les lee libros a los más pequeños en el kindergarten...la maestra de ella la pone a leerles libros a los niños más pequeños, y yo veo que es una gran cosa porque veo que está más sobresaliente en todo a ella siempre la están buscando [para que participe] en actividades, bien activa ella, la más chica.	*My girl [Elena] reads books to the smallest children in the kindergarten...her teacher has her read books to the smallest children, and I see that this is a great thing because I see that she is more outstanding in everything because they are always looking for her to participate in activities, she's very active, the little one.*

A review of Elena's report cards suggested diminished academic performance between Grades 2 and 3. Her report-card grades dropped from mostly Bs in Grade 2 to mostly Cs in Grade 3. However, comments from her teachers during interviews suggested that her academic performance was strengthening, rather than weakening, and that the differences in her grades were due to different grading standards adhered to by teachers from year to year.

Table 2
Children Who Were Successful in School

Child's name	Language at home	Language at school	English proficiency	Literacy at home	Family's attention to school	Literacy at school	English literacy	Spanish literacy	Attitude toward school	Attendance
Beatriz	Spanish and English	English	Fluent	Daily shared and self-initiated reading and writing	Frequently visited school; monitored homework daily	Highly systematic with daily opportunities for extended reading and writing	Above grade level	Above grade level	Excellent attitude and behavior	94%
Belinda	Spanish	Primarily English; some Spanish	Fluent	Daily shared and self-initiated reading and writing	Attended formal school events; monitored homework daily	Highly systematic with daily opportunities for extended reading and writing	On grade level	On grade level	Excellent attitude and behavior	99%
Elena	Spanish and English	English	Fluent	Daily shared and self-initiated reading and writing	Rarely attended school events; monitored homework daily	Highly systematic with daily opportunities for extended reading and writing	On grade level	Unknown	Excellent attitude and behavior	99%

Summary

Table 2 provides a summary of the home and school literacy experiences of Beatriz, Belinda, and Elena. It is evident that there were clear commonalities: They all received strong and consistent support from at least one parent, on a daily or near-daily basis, both in the practice of family literacy and in attention paid to school; all children were explicitly aware of the intergenerational nature of learning between them and their parents; all children were enrolled in classrooms where teachers were perceived to be particularly effective, suggesting strong and consistent learning opportunities; all children had positive attitudes toward school and learning; all had high rates of attendance; and, whether in bilingual or general education classroom settings, all seemed to be learning language in home environments where parents valued and supported proficiency in both Spanish and English. In short, for the children who were experiencing high levels of success, *all* pieces of the academic puzzle were firmly in place.

CHAPTER 4

Children Who Were "On Their Way" to Success in School

In this chapter you will meet five children who were experiencing moderate success in school. Lucho was an 8-year-old boy attending a bilingual second-grade classroom in the public school, and Luisa was his 10-year-old sister attending a fourth-grade bilingual classroom in the same school. Originally from the Dominican Republic, Lucho and Luisa had entered the United States during the second semester of the previous school year. Susana was a 10-year-old child who was born in Puerto Rico and moved to the community during the summer before her fourth-grade year; she had been in a U.S. school for less than a year. Juan, a 9-year-old child, had lived in the United States for 3 years, but had a break in his length of stay when he and his parents returned to Colombia for a year. Ana, an 8-year-old child, had resided in the United States for a total of $6\frac{1}{2}$ years, but, like Juan, these years were marked by a break in her length of stay. At the start of this study, she had just returned to the United States after a $1\frac{1}{2}$-year stay in Puerto Rico.

Juan's mother, Lina, enrolled in the Intergenerational Literacy Project at the time Juan entered third grade. She had completed 10 years of schooling in her country. Juan was the only child in his family. Ana's mother, Sandra, enrolled in the Intergenerational Literacy Project in January of Ana's third-grade year. She had 11 years of education in Puerto Rico. Ana lived at home with her mother, her father, and two younger brothers. Susana's mother, Esmeralda, enrolled in the Intergenerational Literacy Project in October 1994, 3 months after coming to the United States. The year in which the study took place was a difficult one for the family. A few months after moving to the community, the family's apartment was destroyed by fire, and they subsequently moved to a housing project in the same neighborhood. The family also was involved in a car accident in which Susana and her brother Octavio (also a participant in the study) were injured. Lucho and Luisa's father, Bartolomeo, came to the United States first, approximately 3 years before his wife and children. He was a tailor and had 11 years of formal schooling. He enrolled in the Intergenerational Literacy Project in January of Lucho's second-grade year and Luisa's fourth-grade year. Lucho and Luisa's father and Juan's mother described their English proficiency as minimal; Susana's and Ana's mothers described their English proficiency as moderate.

Language at Home and at School

In each of these cases, the children spoke primarily Spanish at home. However, the parents' and children's interest in and motivation for English learning was evident in descriptions of occasions when children used English at home. Juan's mother, for example, explained that family members liked to hear him speak English:

Sí, hablan en mi casa todos [en] español, y él habla en español. A veces cuando hablamos por teléfono [con la familia en Colombia], le dicen a él: "Juan, hablemos en inglés un poquito," y entonces él les habla un poquito en inglés, y ellos no le entienden, pero [se lo piden] sólo por oirlo hablar a él. Les parece bonito.

Yes...everyone in my home speaks Spanish and he speaks in Spanish. Sometimes when we speak to them [family in Colombia] on the phone, they tell him, "Juan, speak to us in English a little." And then he speaks to them in English and they don't understand him, but [they ask] just to hear him speak. They think it's pretty.

Having been in the United States for only 1¹/₂ years, Lucho's dominant language was Spanish. He spoke only Spanish at home and spoke it most of the time at school. His teacher, Ms. Pokorny, reported that Lucho was learning English quickly. His father also commented on his oral English skills, saying that Lucho "speaks more English than the rest."

Luisa said that at home she spoke Spanish most of the time, but with her younger brother, Lucho, she spoke some English. Her teacher, Mrs. Zevallos, described Luisa as a beginning English speaker:

> Luisa is very good in her language. The more dominant a child is in her language the harder it is for her to leave that security and move on to the other language. On the other hand, precisely because she's so good in her language, once she decides "I am going to learn English," she'll do it faster than the others. And that's what is going to happen to Luisa.

She also reported that Luisa's attitude toward learning English had changed since the beginning of the year:

> Her body movement when she gets her English book and...her work production shows that she has lost the fear of the unknown language and that she's OK now. She's not afraid to make mistakes, she's not afraid to come and say, "How can I do blah, blah, blah?" when before she just wouldn't touch, and it's a great deal of fear.

Ana's mother reported that although Ana spoke primarily Spanish at home, she used English with her cousins and her aunt and helped her mother accomplish errands in the community by speaking for her to English-speaking clerks and storekeepers. Sandra described Ana's English speaking skills as limited but improving:

> Entiende lo que le dicen, y lo dice palabras pa[ra] atrás. Y habla con los nenes, pero no habla así mucho. Y escribirlo no sabe, pero sí sabe un poco.

> *She understands what they tell her, and she can answer them. And she speaks to other children, but she doesn't speak a lot. And she doesn't know how to write, but she does know a little.*

Susana said that she did not know English yet but that she was learning. She said that she spoke Spanish at home with her family and at school with her teacher, as well. Her mother, too, described her as speaking mostly Spanish at home, but "a veces, pues, se le sale un poquito en inglés" (*"sometimes, well, a little English slips out"*) because, in her mother's opinion, she was so interested in learning English. Her mother thought that Susana was progressing well in English for the amount of time that she had been in the United States. She said that Susana often interpreted for her.

At school, the children used Spanish most of the time, although each also was said to be increasing the use of English. In evaluating children's, parents', and teachers' attitudes toward the children's development and use of Spanish and English, the evidence suggested that all five children had ample opportunities to both maintain their native language and develop proficiency in English.

Literacy at Home

At home, each of these students participated in shared literacy with at least one of their parents. In three cases, those of Juan, Ana, and Susana, the interactions appeared to be routine and frequent. Juan, for example, reported that he had "lots and lots of books" at home and that many were bilingual: "On top they are in English and on the bottom in Spanish." Both Juan and his mother read together at bedtime each night. Lina identified some favorite books and described in detail the strategies she used when they read together, in this case a prediction strategy: "Yo le leí una parte y yo le pregunté a él, ¿qué va a pasar después de esto?" (*"I read him a part and I asked him, 'What's going to happen after this?'"*).

Both Susana and her mother reported that she spent a good deal of time reading and writing at home. She did this alone, with her mother, and with her brothers. Susana said, for example, that "hay veces que nos sentamos toditos y uno lee una parte y el otro, otra, así" (*"there are times that we all sit down and one of us reads a part, then somebody else, another one, like that"*). Her mother Esmeralda's literacy log entries provided further evidence of her reported frequent literacy activities with her children:

> Read the books tittle [title] *La cara de abuelito* (*Grandpa's Face*), *Where the Wild Things* [Are], *La dama de la luna* (*The Moon Lady*). [literacy log, 11/29/94]

> I read three book [books] *La estatua y el jardincito* (*The Statue and the Little Garden*), *Celiana y la ciudad sumergida* (*Celiana and the Submerged City*), y *La visita de la primavera* (*Spring's Visit*). [literacy log, 3/1/95]

Of 12 literacy log entries in a typical month (November), 6 described help with homework and 5 reported storybook reading. However, this attention to storybook reading seemed to fall off during the summer months. In July, when school was not in session, none of Esmeralda's literacy log entries documented any reading at all.

In Ana's home there was also evidence of frequent shared family literacy activities. Sandra's literacy logs recorded the following events:

Ayude [ayudé] a mis niños aser [a hacer] las tareas. [literacy log, 1/18/95]	*I helped my children with their homework.*
Estudie [Estudié] y le ayude [ayudé] acer [a hacer] las asignaciones a mis niños. [literacy log, 2/15/95]	*I studied and I helped my children do their assignments.*
Leey [leí] un cuento a mis niños y miramos TV. [literacy log, 6/7/95]	*I read a story to my children and we watched TV.*
Leeimos [Leímos] un cuento y hablamos sobre lo que paso [pasó] en el cuento. [literacy log, 6/12/95]	*We read a story and talked about what happened in the story.*

In addition to her literacy interactions with her mother, Ana also read to her younger siblings, as Sandra indicated:

Le lee a mis otros nenes.... Ella coge y a veces les dice que quiere leerles cuentos, y entonces, y viene y sienta a Carlitos en la silla, y se sienta y le lee un cuento, y eso.	*She reads to my other children.... She picks a book and sometimes tells them that she wants to read them a story, and so she comes and she sits Carlitos on a chair and she sits and starts reading him a story and like that.*

In these three families, reading together was not a new family activity; rather, it was something that they had done together before enrolling in the literacy project. However, some differences were noted by the participants. Juan, for example, noticed that his mother read more to him since she started coming to the literacy project. Sandra's literacy teachers commented that during the months of participation in the project, her book-borrowing habits increased substantially. During her interview, Ana, too, commented on her mother's use of the project library:

Cuando ella iba a la escuela, ella cogía libros prestados, ¿verdad? Ella se los llevaba pa(ra) la casa, y ella a veces me los leía a mí, y a veces yo le digo, "Mami, ¿puedo coger este libro para leerlo?" Y ella me dice: "Sí." Y yo lo cogía y [lo] leía.	*When she went to school, she would borrow books, right? She would bring them home, and she would sometimes read them to me, and sometimes I would tell her, "Sweety, can I borrow this book to read?" And she would tell me "Yes." And I would take it and read it.*

Susana's mother, Esmeralda, reported that the amount of reading she did with her children had not changed, but that the ways she read and the interactions she had with her children around books did. As a result, she explained, the children were increasingly choosing to reread stories to her after she had read to them.

Pues que, como te digo, que hay veces que cuando yo me siento a leer con ellos, hay veces pues yo les leo, ellos me dicen, "Ay, déjame leerlo a mí," y antes no hacían nada de eso.	*Well, like I've been telling you that there are times when I sit down to read with them, there are times, well, I read to them, they say to me, "Hey, let me read it," and they never did anything like that before.*

Aside from reading together, participants in these three families also reported writing together, mostly letters to distant relatives. In addition, however, writing was done for practical and recreational reasons, such as the following example from Ana's case:

Ayer me hizo una carta, ¿verdad? Me puso corazoncitos. Eran dos, ¿verdad? En el primero me escribió: "Mami, I love you," que si te quiero, que si esto, que si lo otro. Y entonces, después en la próxima me dijo: "Mami, pa[ra] ir a Haymarket hay que coger la gua-gua 111." Porque quiere ir a un sitio, yo no sé que lío…un sitio en Boston, parece que deber de haber algo, porque me dijo: "Mami, tienes que coger la gua-gua ésta" y me pone	*Yesterday she wrote me a letter, right? She drew little hearts. There were two, right? On the first, she wrote, "Mommy, I love you," that I love you, this and that. And then, on the other one, she wrote, "Mommy, to get to Haymarket, you have to take the number 111 bus." Because she wants to go to some place, I don't know where…some place in Boston…it seems that there must be something going on, because*

<table>
<tr>
<td>"sí o no," tú sabes, si "sí o no" la iba a llevar.</td>
<td>she wrote, "Mami, you have to take this bus," and she wrote, "Yes or No," you know, "Yes or No," if I would take her.</td>
</tr>
</table>

In Juan's home, family members wrote notes as a way of sharing emotions:

<table>
<tr>
<td>Yo le escribo a él y le digo yo, "Mi gordito lindo, mi lindo precioso," [con] dibujitos, [o] "¿qué día es?" Por la mañana cuando no se ha levantado, yo le escribo "tan lindo mi gordito, ¿cómo amaneció mi niño? y así. Todo lo que él hace, a mí me gusta, y yo lo animo…. Yo me siento bien, lo mismo que el papá…. El llega y "Papi, te traje un regalito," y le muestra una carta: "Te quiero mucho, Ud., mi papá, mi mamá, y yo somos una familia," y así.</td>
<td>I write to him and I say to him, "My chubby little boy, my precious child," [with] little drawings, [or] "what day is it?" In the morning before he gets up, I write to him, "My chubby little boy, how are you this morning?" And like that. Everything he makes for me, I like it and I encourage him…. I feel good and so does his father…. He comes home and [Juan says] "Dad, I brought you a small present!" and he shows him a letter [that says] "I love you very much. You, my father, my mother, and I are a family," like that.</td>
</tr>
</table>

As with the children who were found to be highly successful in school, both Juan and Ana commented on the intergenerational benefits of their shared literacy experiences with their parents. The following example provided by Lina, Juan's mother, is representative:

<table>
<tr>
<td>El me dice cuando llega de la escuela, "Mami, aprendí tal cosa, repita conmigo en inglés." Y yo repito con él.</td>
<td>He says to me when he comes back from school, "Mommy, I learned this—repeat it with me in English." And I repeat with him.</td>
</tr>
</table>

In Lucho and Luisa's case, data did not provide a clear picture of literacy at home. Bartolomeo did report that he read with them and that since he received a library card, he sometimes took his children to the library, but that his wife tended to do so more frequently.

<table>
<tr>
<td>A nosotros nos dieron las tarjetas por vía del proyecto. Entonces yo</td>
<td>We received the library card through the project, so I always</td>
</tr>
</table>

| siempre voy con ellos. Ella (la mamá) va más con ellos, unas dos horas. | *go with them. She [the mother] goes more with them, she goes for about two hours.* |

Luisa and Lucho both mentioned that they and their father shared books that he brought home from school. Luisa named several books, such as *La oruguita muy hambrienta* (*The Very Hungry Caterpillar*), *El perro grande rojo*, (*The Big Red Dog*), *El autobús mágico*, (*The Magic Bus*), and her phonics book.

However, their father Bartolomeo's literacy log entries primarily document what he did at work (mending and making clothes) and the ways he practiced literacy on his own. His entries on the side of the form asking about shared literacy activities primarily report that he took his children to school. He did on a few occasions record that he read to his children, spent time with them, and that they did "commentaries" together. When asked about these activities, he offered few additional details. Although the events cited are valuable and important, there are relatively few references to such activities. During his literacy class, Bartolomeo spoke little of his children's academic efforts and only occasionally commented on their schoolwork or school behaviors.

Each of these five children engaged in frequent self-initiated literacy activities at home. Lucho said that he read at home, mostly books that he brought from school, and his father also said he "wrote a lot." Luisa said that she read and wrote at home when she played school, one of her favorite play scenarios. Her mother, too, was apparently active in these play activities:

| Cuando estoy jugando con mi hermano a la maestra, que le hago disque cartas a mi mamá para que ellos se la lleven, ella me lo firma y cuando ellos van disque a la escuela pues me la dan. | *When I am playing teacher with my brother, I make so-called letters for my mother so that they take them to her, she signs them and they go to the so-called school and they give them to me.* |

Ana mentioned her interest in writing at home: "A veces yo escribo cuentos.... Yo escribo de las cosas que a mí me gustan, de los colores preferidos de mi mamá, cuál es la ropa que a ella le gusta mucho" (*"Sometimes I write stories.... I write about the things that I like, about my mother's favorite colors, what clothes she really likes"*).

Susana explained that after doing her homework each day, she generally read or wrote on her own.

Leo un poco, descanso un poco, mmm, como no puedo jugar pero, pero puedo jugar con un papel o algo así, pues, pues me pongo a escribir cosas o leo. Escribo a mis abuelas o [a] mi familia en Puerto Rico, mmhmm.	*I read a little, take a break, mmm, since I can't play, but, but I can play with paper or something, well, well, I start to write things, or, or I read. I write to my grandmothers or my family in Puerto Rico, mmhmm.*

She said that she preferred chapter books, especially about Snow White and Peter Pan and that she often chose to read in English. "En inglés, más me gusta leer porque así estoy aprendiendo palabras, esas cosas, así" (*"I prefer to read in English because then I learn more words, stuff like that"*). Finally, Juan's mother said he enjoyed reading by himself: "El lee, coge un libro y le da por leer, lo lee alto, lee duro…solo en la pieza" (*"He reads, he picks up a book when he feels like reading, he reads out loud. He reads loud by himself…in his room"*).

Family's Attention to School

Although attention to school in these families was clearly evident, the ways in which parents were involved varied. For the most part, all parents visited the classroom frequently and were involved with children's homework activities and behavior at school. Ana's mother, for example, met with the teacher almost daily, checked and helped her with homework, and even assigned homework when the teacher did not:

A veces no le dan asignaciones, y cuando no le dan asignaciones, pues ella no se quiere sentar a estudiar. Yo siempre le digo: "Ana, cuando uno viene de la escuela, uno repasa todo lo que le dieron en la escuela."	*Sometimes they don't give her homework, and when they don't, well, she doesn't want to sit and study. I always tell her, "Ana, when you come from school, you have to review everything they gave you in school."*

Ana's teacher regarded Sandra as a concerned and supportive parent whose participation in her child's schooling had been consistent throughout the year.

Her mother has been very cooperative. She is always communicating with me and she's always asking me about how she is doing, and I, I think, that her mother is very, is very attentive to her needs, and every time we've been talking about her reading and her writing she helps her a lot.

Juan's mother also attended to and monitored Juan's schooling. Juan's second-grade teacher, Ms. Gómez, remembered Lina as a concerned mother who would contact her on a daily basis to inquire about her son's "general progress and behavior." Mrs. Hernández, Juan's third-grade teacher, also described Lina as "cooperative" and said that Lina met with her regularly, "always asking me how she can help" with Juan's homework.

Lina's literacy log entries provided further evidence of her involvement in Juan's schoolwork. Most of the entries about literacy events shared with her child described how she helped him with his homework:

Hoy le ayude [ayudé] a mi niño [a] hacer su tarea antes de venir aca [acá] y lo deje [dejé] con su papá y le [se] quedo [quedó] haciendo dibujos y pintando y leyendo libros de ingles [inglés] y español. [literacy log, 3/27/95]

Today I helped my son do his homework before coming here and I left him with his daddy and he stayed making pictures and painting and reading books in English and Spanish.

Hoy dia [día] le ayude [ayudé] a hacer a mi hijo su tarea para el dia [día] siguiente. Se trataba de como [cómo] diferenciar los animales y como [cómo] son ellos y que [qué] comen. Yo le di una idea sobre los peses [peces] como [cómo] vivían en el agua y q' [qué] comían y como [cómo] eran ellos. de q' [qué] colores y le parecio [pareció] muy bonito luego me pidio [pidió] el favor de que le enseñara a como [cómo] hacer macaronis en chis y le enseñe ahora el [él] mismo los prepara solo. [literacy log, 3/2/95]

Today I helped my son do his homework for the day. Next he tried to distinguish animals and how they are and what they eat. I gave him an idea about fish how they lived in the water what they ate and what colors and it looked very pretty later he asked me to do the favor of teaching him how to make macaroni and cheese and I taught him now he can prepare it all by himself.

Lucho and Luisa's father described different types of school interactions for each child. Because Lucho at times experienced behavior difficulties, this issue was most salient in both interviews and Bartolomeo's literacy log entries:

Dialogar con mi hijo hacerca [acerca] de la escuela.	*Talk to my son about school.* [literacy log, 1/26/95]
Tener dialogo [diálogo] acerca de como [cómo] comportarce [comportarse] en la escuela.	*Have dialogue about how to behave in school.* [literacy log, 1/31/95]

Both his father and his teacher explained that his mother talked with the teacher "every couple of weeks" to check on his behavior. Ms. Pokorny commented,

We've been working together and talking to him and talking to the mother, and talking to the father a little bit but mostly the mother. The mother seems to be the one who comes. The father came but, I don't want to say that he wasn't interested, but I don't think that he thought that it was a big issue. And the mother is very concerned; she really wants to see him doing well.

Although Ms. Pokorny expressed concern about Lucho's attention to his schoolwork, she believed that his reasonably good rate of progress was an indicator of the support he was getting at home:

It does seem like somebody must be doing something with him at home, because, despite the fact that I would say a third of the day he may not be focusing with us, he's still doing pretty well; he's still reading well, he's still writing well. So it seems to me that someone must be reading with him at home, because he even came in with pretty good reading skills for a second grader. And he likes to read, he likes to kind of talk about the book, he'll say, "What happened, can you tell me?" You know, "describe the story." You know, he'll like to participate in that part of the literacy block.

In Luisa's case, her parents reported that she did well in school, and they apparently did not perceive a need to stay in contact with the teacher. Luisa's homework was given special attention and was monitored daily. In his interview, for example, Bartolomeo explained that there was a special homework time that lasted for 2 hours. Luisa also said that sometimes when she did not know something, she received help from her parents. She gave a particular example of a time when they helped her with math because she was having problems with division.

Mrs. Zevallos, Luisa's teacher, commented on the infrequent contact between her and the family:

> I think it's interesting that her mother hasn't come in any of my PTO sessions. And even when the parents are all the time reminded that we're going to have PTO on such and such a day between such and such hours, I have only seen the mother twice and because I call her, or send a note to say to come see me. But again I have to say, in all fairness to this family, that this is the standard in my class.

However, Mrs. Zevallos also reported that when Luisa started to fall behind, she contacted her mother and she did make a point to come in to see her daughter's teacher after that:

> [I] saw the mother this morning…. I had called her to come and see me and this was something that has taken her 1 week to comply with. Her excuses seem quite legitimate I must say…. She could not come because she had appointments and [another] child…. She's always very pleasant and very happy to come when she can.

Susana's mother reported that she did not generally attend formal school functions, but that she did pick up Susana at school every day and routinely checked with her teacher then. Both Susana and her mother reported that Susana completed her homework as soon as she arrived home from school each day and that her mother helped her whenever necessary. For instance, Esmeralda said, "Y ahora ella sabe más, porque ella las tareas ya las hace sola" (*"And now she knows more because she does her homework by herself"*). Susana commented,

Yo prefiero hacerlo sola. Entonces, si yo tengo alguna duda o algo, pues, yo voy y le pregunto a mi mamá, porque es mejor así, porque uno aprende más, porque si la mamá está, "Esto es aquí, esto es acá, esto es acá, esto está mal." A mí me gusta que mi mamá me ayude.	*I prefer to do it alone. Then if I'm not sure or something, well, I go and ask my mom because it's better that way because you learn more and it's better because if mom is around, "This goes here, that goes there, that goes there, this is wrong." I like when my mom helps.*

Ms. Elkins, Susana's teacher, said that she believed that Esmeralda was supportive of Susana and that she saw "a bond" between the parents and the child in terms of her schooling: "they want her to do her best."

Child's Attitude Toward School

With regard to motivation toward school and learning, all students were described positively. Ana and Susana were described as motivated students and as being particularly interested in reading and writing in both English and Spanish. Although generally positive, some unevenness in motivation was portrayed in Juan's, Luisa's, and Lucho's cases.

Ana was described as a student who liked school so much she begged to go even when she was very sick. Her mother Sandra said:

A ella no le gusta faltar, aunque esté enferma. Mira antier, ella estaba por la noche con un dolor de cabeza y vomitando, con dolor de estómago, con fiebre y todo, y me decía, lo único que me decía era: "Mami, yo mañana quiero ir para la escuela."	*She doesn't like to miss school even when she's sick. Look, 2 days ago, she had a headache, and she was vomiting, with a stomachache, fever, everything. And she would say to me, the only thing she would say was, "Mommy, tomorrow I want to go to school."*

Mrs. Hernández, Ana's teacher, also regarded her as a very good student who was responsible about the work she turned in. She finished her work on time and was an active participant in the classroom:

She's very responsible, very responsible. She finishes her work on time, clean, clear...she's great, she's a very good student. In terms of behavior, she is very kind, she is very sweet. She is very shy...but now...she is a good participant in our classroom.

According to Mrs. Hernández during her second interview, Ana's motivation was consistent throughout the school year. She said, "Comparing her with other students in my classroom, she has improved and she tries hard. She really wants to learn."

Susana's teacher observed that she frequently self-initiated reading in both Spanish and English and that she was particularly interested in writing: "She writes in her journal more than any other student in the class." In her interview, Susana was clear about liking school. When asked what she liked best about school, she said, "Me gusta todo, todo, todo, todo, todo" (*"I like it all, all, all, all, all"*). According to Ms. Elkins, Susana had never missed a homework assignment. She rated Susana as the lowest in the class in English proficiency but the highest in motivation. She said that Susana asked for extra help when she needed it. Although some of the other students in her class made fun of Susana early in the year because she spoke so quickly in Spanish, she worked well with the other students.

Comments about Juan's attitude, motivation, and behavior in school were also generally positive. His second-grade teacher described him as a verbal, outgoing child. She recalled that "his effort, the effort grade is here [referring to his report card], A's. He was a hard worker. He tried hard. I mean, he was a little mischievous, but he was a hard worker." These comments were similar to those on his report card from Colombia, in which he was portrayed as responsible, respecting of others, and a child with excellent oral communication skills.

However, his third-grade teacher, Mrs. Hernández, also described him as verbal and outgoing, but for her, these attributes seemed to have become negative. She said, "He likes...to talk...to his friends and it's interrupting and distracting." Her remarks about Juan suggested that his school behavior might have been somewhat erratic. At times during the interviews, she described very positive behaviors, saying that Juan was "motivated," "responsible with his homework," and "wants to learn." She also noted that Juan often selected a book to read with a friend and that he loved to take books home to read. But at other times she seemed to contradict these comments, perhaps recalling a particular incident. She described Juan as "not always on task," "very lazy," and noted that "you have to push him to work." She concluded in the final interview that "He's been working better, but he could do better."

In the cases of Lucho and Luisa, we received inconsistent portrayals of their attitude toward school. Lucho was described to be an enthusiastic learner "under certain circumstances." During his interview, Lucho reported that he liked to go to school: "A mí me gusta ir a la escuela porque aprendo mucho" (*"I like to go to school because I learn a lot"*). His teacher, Ms. Pokorny, said that "he's very bright,

and when he's engaged, [he] can do some really beautiful work...."
Based on her description, Lucho was a high-achieving child who enjoyed learning, as long as he was having fun. She went on to say the
following:

> I think that he wants to do well, I think that he wants to please the
> teacher, he wants to please his parents, he wants to be proud of himself,
> but at the same time, I think that he doesn't necessarily do what he con-
> siders to be "work." So, if he considers that it's a fun activity, or that he's
> going to do real well and you're going to be happy, and he's going to be
> happy, he likes it. But I don't know, he doesn't like to work. But he
> likes it, like I said, he likes to discuss things, because he's very articulate
> so that he can talk about the book and he feels very, not even like he's
> working, it just kind of comes naturally from him.

She continued a few minutes later:

> He's very enthusiastic when he likes something. He's very talented ar-
> tistically...he likes to help the teacher, he wants to clean my desk, he
> wants to clean the floor, he wants to do whatever.

Yet, on the other hand, there were times when Lucho experienced
serious difficulties. These problems were centered around the display
of aggression and impulsivity. At one point, for example, he was
banned from riding the school bus because he was hitting students on
the bus. His way of behaving, Ms. Pokorny said, influenced his work:

> If it weren't for his behavior, he'd be a great, great student. He's very
> smart.... He always wants to take his time on things instead of rushing
> through them. He always wants to make sure it's perfect before he hands
> it in. And actually, he gets angry sometimes if we don't have that extra
> time and that will cause a problem, because he just wants everything to
> be perfect.

She went on to explain how Lucho's display of aggression did not
seem to be specific to the school setting, and his family, especially
his mother, was concerned about it:

> The mother was very concerned when she came in, I mean she stayed for
> like an hour and a half one day, just saying, "Oh my goodness, yes, we
> have this problem in the house too." But I know that the mother is real-
> ly trying. She came on the field trip and everything because that was
> the only way he was allowed to go.

Ms. Pokorny reported that a social worker had been working with Lucho and with her to help correct his behavior difficulties. Ms. Pokorny believed that this intervention was helping him learn how to communicate his negative feelings more effectively.

A final comment on Lucho's attitude toward school was found in the researcher's field notes detailing an April interview with Ms. Pokorny. The researcher recorded the following:

> After the interview, Ms. Pokorny went to her classroom to get Lucho's report card and came back with a note he had written to her during the interview. It was in Spanish and said that he liked her and liked school and there was a drawing. She [Ms. Pokorny] was very touched and said she was glad he liked school "today"—she mentioned a few times how his motivation/desire seems to come and go.

Like her brother, Luisa indicated that she liked school. When asked what she liked to do after school, Luisa said, "Mis tareas y salir a jugar" (*"My homework and go out to play"*), indicating an interest in and conscientiousness about her schoolwork. Her father, too, portrayed her as motivated and hardworking:

Ella lee bastante y hace todos los ejercicios cuando ella llega de la clase hasta que hace todos los ejercicios. Uno los deja una, dos horas después de clase.	*She reads a lot and does all her homework when she arrives from school until she finishes all her work. One leaves them for about 1, 2 hours after school.*

Mrs. Zevallos's observations, on the other hand, suggested somewhat less motivation and enthusiasm for school than these comments imply. When asked about Luisa's attitude toward school, Mrs. Zevallos said the following:

> I have about six children that are truly bilingual—not up to the fourth grade, but they're bilingual, let's say up to third grade level both in English and in Spanish. She could do as well in her Spanish as this more advanced group within the class, but somehow she's not. She's staying with the other group that is a little lower. Her projects in social studies and science could be better. They [her family] seem to spend a lot of time in the church. So that must take time in her evenings. Luisa gives the overall impression to be a very good little mother, a very good little sister, a very good social being, but is not a child that is achieving in the studies. She seems to be very strong in social skills, but not as much in

the study skills. You know what I mean? Like she seems very mature when it concerns social issues but not academic issues and that's the transition that I'm trying to help her with. That it is wonderful to be in charge of the food shopping, or who has to go and get lunch, but it's very important that she assumes that studying and learning is something we choose to do and that no matter how much I can coach her…it is truly something she has to make a decision. She is listening to what I say. And there have been some signs that she's beginning to buy it, but not yet. Often I feel that if I have Luisa for another year, she will totally blossom.

At the time of her second interview, Mrs. Zevallos's concerns about Luisa had increased, and in response she had contacted Luisa's mother. Mrs. Zevallos said, "Luisa was falling dramatically behind and I was very concerned that her work was just nonexistent. Her homework was badly done, only some of it…her attitude seemed to go back to earlier weeks in September." After contacting Luisa's mother, however, Luisa's school behavior became more focused and consistent and remained so through the end of the school year.

Literacy at School

All of these children were in bilingual classrooms. Teachers' reports of their instructional routines suggested that in all cases, the children were receiving reasonably intensive Spanish literacy instruction and that they were in classrooms in which time allocated to English language and literacy instruction was increasing gradually.

Ana and Juan's third-grade teacher, Mrs. Hernández, was a native Spanish speaker who was originally from Puerto Rico. In this school, children were assigned to bilingual classes on the basis of high or low English proficiency. Mrs. Hernández's class was intended for children with lower English proficiency. A Chapter 1 Spanish reading teacher also worked in Mrs. Hernández's class. Although Ana was identified as eligible for Chapter 1 reading support, there was no indication that she worked individually or in a small group with the Chapter 1 teacher.

Mrs. Hernández explained that she provided a number of opportunities for the children in her class to learn and practice literacy in both Spanish and English, although most instruction was conducted in

Spanish. The following dialogue provided a snapshot of some of the ways children read and wrote in Spanish:

Mrs. Hernández: Oh yes, they have to read every morning when they come to school, to my room.

Interviewer: Is that material they choose themselves?

Mrs. Hernández: They, they choose. They choose, and then, they write their log, their reading log, and then, they write a little summary about what they have read.

Interviewer: And they do that every morning?

Mrs. Hernández: Every morning...and they have to write. They have to write a story, a math story every day...at home. A problem using a concept that we have been doing in the classroom. Also they have to read social studies.

In English, Mrs. Hernández focused on helping students develop word-attack skills in the context of what they were reading:

I started giving them clusters, letter clusters...how to drop the *e*'s and how to, how to, consonant, blank, consonant digraph. That helped them to write, to read because they couldn't. Spanish is very phonetic, so each word, each letter has a sound. Not in English. So I started to give them a lot of that, and in context. Reading a story and pulling some words and discussing and giving them vocabulary and vocabulary and vocabulary. But I started with things that we use daily. For example, I started with clothing, colors, school things, and reading paragraph, reading and then pulling, integrating again, describing adjectives. So giving them a lot of vocabulary to build up. But now they can write using the, the structure of the language correctly.

In addition, Mrs. Hernández explained that children were supposed to read for a half hour at home. Each Friday, students were asked to submit summaries of what they had read during the week.

Mrs. Hernández described Ana as an "independent reader" and excellent student. Nonetheless, she did express some concern about Ana's rate of progress: "She's having some problems reading. She doesn't read fluently. She is stuck." Sandra was aware of her daughter Ana's difficulties and attempted to support Ana's school learning by having her read and practice at home:

Tú sabes, que como está mal en lectura, yo le digo: "Ana, ponte a leer." Entonces, ella coge su libro y empieza como el papagallo: "aurrurururu." A las millas comienza a leer el cuento, y "Mami, ya estudié." No pasan ni algunos, mira, ni diez minutos pasan, y ella dice: "Mami yo ya estudié," porque a veces no le dan asignaciones, y cuando no le dan asignaciones, pues ella no se quiere sentar a estudiar. Yo siempre le digo: "Ana, cuando uno viene de la escuela, uno repasa todo lo que le dieron en la escuela," tú sabes, para que se le quede algo. Entonces, a ella no le gusta hacer eso.

You know, because she's not doing well in reading, I tell her, "Ana, go read." So, she takes her book, and she starts like a parrot: "aurrururururu." At the speed of light, she begins to read the story, and: "Mami, I already studied." Not even a few, listen, not even 10 minutes go by, and she is saying, "Mami, I already studied," because sometimes she doesn't have homework, and when they don't give her any homework, well, she doesn't want to study. I always tell her, "Ana, when one comes back from school, one needs to review what was taught that day at school," you know, so that one retains something. She doesn't like doing that.

Ana's writing skills were portrayed similarly by Mrs. Hernández. She said, "She has improved her writing, but still is having some...problems." Despite these difficulties, Mrs. Hernández spoke specifically of the ways Ana excelled in writing: "[She] loves to write, mhmm, to write stories. She knows now how to do the elements of the story."

In the final interview, Mrs. Hernández reported that Ana had made excellent progress in Spanish reading, progressing from a second-grade level in February to a beginning third-grade level by June. In English reading, she also had made good progress, progressing from a first-grade level in February to a second-grade level at the end of the year. When asked what changes she had noticed in Ana, Mrs. Hernández said: "Ana has improved a lot.... Ana is one of my best students right now." On her final report card, she achieved satisfactory marks in both academic learning and conduct.

When describing Juan's reading performance, Mrs. Hernández reported that Juan struggled with reading and writing. She said, "His

reading is low...he's not reading fluently...his writing is improving."
Mrs. Hernández also observed that despite his apparent difficulty,
Juan "loves to take books and read."

Juan's second-grade teacher also observed that he really enjoyed
reading and recalled that he often would select picture books with a
friend. She described his Spanish reading ability as "fair" and said that
although he was not a fluent reader, he was reading at an appropriate
level. She also said that his Spanish writing ability "lagged behind"
his peers. During the two quarters that he was in this teacher's classroom, he received A's and Bs on his report cards. Writing also was
identified as an area of concern by his teacher in Colombia, who recommended on his report card that his parents work on writing at
home. Report-card comments also praised his oral language skills and
his delivery of ideas during class.

In the final interview, Mrs. Hernández noted that, although Juan
was not reading at grade level, he had made good progress in Spanish
reading: "He's reading better, now he is reading more smoothly. "She
also reported that he was reading very simple English materials. Juan's
final report card grades were mostly Ps, indicating that he was progressing in his acquisition of all assessed skills in literacy and content
areas. He was described as "inconsistent" in his ability to spell, to respond to text in writing or through drawings, and in organizing his
ideas for writing. In addition, his report card also shows some inconsistent behaviors, such as following rules and displaying self-control.

Lucho received instruction in reading and writing in both Spanish and English. Spanish literacy instruction was offered during the afternoon. Ms. Pokorny described routine activities:

> And then after lunch we have writing time, and we do a different kind of
> writing every day. Sometimes it will just be a kind of like process writ-
> ing and they'll be writing about something they've experienced or some-
> thing they're thinking about. Or other times it will be, I'll read a story and
> they'll have to write problem-solution or they'll write their own stories,
> so we kind of vary the writing time. And the last period we have litera-
> cy. He reads, we basically follow the model, so we have, we'll one day do
> the introduction to the story and the background and predictions and all
> that. And then the children will read it silently. And then the next day, typ-
> ically, it would be the partner reading and then guided reading questions
> they can work with. And then, you know, the activities would vary a lit-
> tle more, but he's reading during the literacy block every day.

English reading instruction was conducted during the daily ESL time, and Ms. Pokorny perceived Lucho as one of the higher achievers in the class in English reading:

> During English, Lucho works with me—he's in my ESL group which is the higher group; we divide it up according to level of ability in English, because my group is reading in English, and the other group isn't. So he's reading right now in English, and doing a pretty good job. I mean obviously he's still on maybe a first-grade level, because it's English, but he's doing a really good job.

Ms. Pokorny observed that Lucho read well in groups and independently, pointing out that he enjoyed reading and chose to read in his free time. She said, "He'll say to me a lot of the time if he finishes his work, 'Can I get a book?' And so that's a good thing. He does like to read."

Ms. Pokorny also commented on Lucho's interest in writing, but she pointed out that he sometimes needed to be coaxed into writing during his spare time:

> He also, he'll want to take a piece of paper and draw…then I'll say to him too, you know, "Can you write about what you drew?" And he'll do that, you know, sometimes you kind of hook him in from what he really wants to do and then you get him to do it. And we just made, actually, books with the lift. We read a book and it was a lift-up flap, *Where's My Egg?* and we looked under things and everything and then we made our own. And he finished his with everyone, and then he was like, "Well, can I make another page? Can I do more?" So, I mean, like I said, he's very enthusiastic when he's hooked into it, when he's interested.

By the second interview, Ms. Pokorny noticed some positive changes in Lucho's attitude toward and uses of writing in the classroom. She said, "The main thing I have noticed was that…he started doing a lot more writing and just, you know, writing me notes, writing notes, writing in his journal—he's really beginning to like to write."

Overall, Lucho was judged to be a solid reader and writer. However, his inconsistent motivation and attitude affected his school literacy performance. Ms. Pokorny summarized how she viewed Lucho's overall literacy performance:

> It's kind of erratic. I mean there are things that he does that are just phenomenal; they're better than most of the things I receive, like writing

assignments, or books. I wish I could show you the books that he did, 'cause that kind of would show you. It's really, really good for a second grader. Other times, he'll do things that are just not, no effort has gone into it and it's very obvious. So again, it comes down to, I guess, the effort and the attitude and all that…sometimes, he'll give me really great things and sometimes he'll give me things with just one word and just no effort and doesn't want to do it and isn't going to do it, and so it's kind of a hard decision to say like how he compares, because it just kind of depends on the day or the assignment or…. Capability-wise, I would say he's upper-average…so he's making good progress, he's reading well, he's writing well, he's doing well with math, but he's not an "A" student, as you would say, or whatever. And I think that…if he were focused and if he were putting the effort, he may very well be.

Despite the teacher's clear impressions of Lucho as a very good reader and writer, his father, Bartolomeo, was under the impression that Lucho did not read as well as the teacher indicated, although he was aware of his steady progress. He said the following:

Siempre me mandaban a decir de la escuela que estaba un poco flojo en lectura. Entonces, parece que puso un poco más de esfuerzo, porque como casi no sabe leer, como en cuestión de dos meses aprendió pronto, parece como que el puso énfasis y se desarrolló bastante. La profesora me dijo que ya estaba bien en la lectura que ya estaba leyendo bien.	*They would sometimes tell me that he was a little behind in reading, so it seems he tried harder because he doesn't know how to read. In about 2 months, he learned. It seemed he put emphasis on this and developed this area. The teacher told me that he was doing well in reading, that he was reading better.*

Bartolomeo also seemed to be unclear about the purpose of the bilingual program, apparently viewing Lucho's placement in Spanish reading as evidence that he was not doing well:

A él lo ponen a leer en español porque no está muy pulido en la lectura, pero ya le cogió el ritmo y lo hace mejor.	*They put him to read in Spanish because he is not too polished in reading, but he got the hang of it and is doing better.*

Like her brother, Luisa also enjoyed participating in literacy activities and was a solid reader and writer in Spanish. At the end of third grade, Luisa received A's and Bs for the final quarter on her report card. At that time, she was judged to be achieving grade-level proficiency in Spanish reading and preprimer level proficiency in English reading. Her grades diminished a bit in fourth grade, but she was generally judged to be making good academic progress. She finished the year earning Bs in both Spanish and English reading and Cs in other academic subjects. The final achievement levels recorded by her teacher on her report card indicated grade-appropriate performance in Spanish reading and second-grade performance in English reading.

Reading instruction in Luisa's class was conducted in English. Mrs. Zevallos described a typical class:

> Mrs. Zevallos: We read every day in our basal reader, that again is 1.5 [reading level]. The teacher, myself, models the reading. The children then read a paragraph each. When we have completed the reading, we go over new words in the reader. I call their attention to say, um, patterns in the reading, the present tense of the verb, the past tense, irregular of the verb, whether there are antonyms or whatever new aspect of the language art is in the reading, we go over it. The children then are assigned some about 10 or 12 words for spelling. I then read the story again to them. And that becomes their homework. I also read...
>
> Interviewer: To read the story again themselves?
>
> Mrs. Zevallos: Ah ha. Then the next day we read the same story again, but now our approach is different. We now ask questions: What is the story about? Who are the characters in the story? Did you like this story? Why did you like this story? And I try to coach them a little bit to use as many words as possible, but sometimes if the child is able to put it all back in himself or herself, then I let it be. When they are at a loss for a word, I help them out.

Mrs. Zevallos explained that there were significant differences in Luisa's academic performance in Spanish and in English. She said that when Luisa was able to use her first language, she did well and liked to participate:

> In Spanish, she participates 100%. In this class her homework and her completion of work is excellent in Spanish. She's a very good student and she's also a very bright child, but she's a bit stubborn to learn English and her participation was really very minimal in September, October, and a lot of push, push, push and then after January, February she really began to work more on it and now I would say that she's in the 65%–75% participation. So considering where she was and where she is now, she has done a lot.

However, during English reading time, the teacher noted that, like many children, Luisa

> was very much afraid because she's very proud. She didn't want to hear herself making any mistakes. It took a lot of encouragement and a lot of applause to say, "See how well you're doing, see how well you sound." Then she began to smile, but her fears and her reluctance to make mistakes I think were her handicap and we are overcoming.

Mrs. Zevallos also commented more generally on Luisa's interest and enthusiasm for reading:

> Luisa's eager to go to our, we have a little library that we put together because the school doesn't have a library time. I've decided that library time is very, very important so I organized a little library and the children every Friday get books so that during the weekend they can have books. Luisa would pick up three, four, five books easily. She loves to read, but, of course, in Spanish. If I asked her, "Ah this is not very hard in English—do you want to read it?" She'd say " Oh, ya, ya" and I notice it's left on the table.

During the interview, Luisa demonstrated the interest her teacher spoke of. She brought a book from her classroom that she was reading in English and eagerly read a selection from it to the interviewer.

There was little mention of how Luisa wrote at school. Luisa, herself, reported that "A mí me gusta escribir, pero no mucho" (*"I like to write, but not too much"*).

As in the previous cases, Susana was making steady progress in reading and writing and showed enthusiasm when participating in these activities. Her third-grade report card from Puerto Rico was not available nor was any information about her third-grade year. In fourth grade, Ms. Elkins reported that reading and writing were incorporated into each subject throughout the school day. She explained that in social studies, which was conducted in English, the students worked individually or in groups and read trade books, which were available in English and Spanish. Susana had chosen to read books in Spanish and lower level books in English and by so doing was able to keep up with the class.

Ms. Elkins also said that approximately 1 hour of the school day was devoted to reading instruction, with an additional 20 minutes of sustained silent reading time. Reading groups were shared with another class, and Susana began the year in the lower reading group that was led by the other teacher. She was in the higher group for the second half of the year, however, because she did not enjoy the other group and asked her teacher to let her switch.

> I said, "OK, well, maybe you can. You need to try really hard," but that's…we're at a different level of reading and I try to give her easier stuff, but she is reading at the…basically at the same level with them with a lower comprehension. Lower comprehension, I am sure, but with all the talks we have about it in both languages, I think she's grasping a lot.

Ms. Elkins said that Susana frequently self-initiated reading and often chose picture books in English. Her reading was improving and, by the end of the school year, Ms. Elkins noted that Susana had told her that she was beginning to understand what she read in English.

> She told me, she came to school a couple of weeks ago, she was like, "Ms. Elkins, Ms. Elkins, I, I was reading." I don't know, I forgot what she told me she was reading, but she was reading something in English, she was like, "I understood everything." And she was so excited.

Susana reported reading in both Spanish and English in school and said that when she read in English, "hablamos o la maestra me lo traduce o yo entiendo un poquito" (*"we talk or the teacher translates it for me, or I understand a little"*).

Ms. Elkins reported that the class wrote summaries or reactions to reading nearly every day. She described Susana as a "prolific writer in Spanish; she gets her ideas down, then revises and edits." Ms. Elkins recalled that she initiated a letter to a classmate in the hospital and that she wrote more in her journal than any other student in the class. She also commented on the change in Susana's writing. She said that at the beginning of the year, she only copied dictations in English, but she was now beginning to write her own ideas as well.

Susana also reported that she wrote in her journal every day, responding to a question that the teacher had put on the board. She also discussed a story that she wrote in Spanish. When asked about writing in English, she provided the following description:

Bueno, la maestra dice, "Escribe tal cosa, pues, nosotros la escribimos …[hay veces] los nenes me ayudan o la maestra para poder poner las cosas que hice bien y las cosas que hice mal. Y después las cosas que hice mal, pues, ellos me ayudan para ponerlas bien, y me dicen, "Esto, esto se lee así o se escribe así, pues yo lo escribo."	*Well, the teacher says, "Write such and such, and, well, we write it…[sometimes] the kids help me or the teacher so I can put down the things I did right and the things I did wrong. And afterwards, well, they help me correct the things I did wrong, and they say, "This, this you read like this or you write like this, and then I write it."*

Susana's report cards indicated good progress in reading. In Spanish reading, she received three A's and a B for the four quarters and was reported to be reading on grade level. In English reading, she received an A for the first marking period, Bs for the second and third periods, and a B- for the final period. Her reading level in English was described as 1.0 for the first marking period and 1.2 for the second quarter; there were no levels reported for the final two marking periods. In English language, her grades were A, B, A-, and B over the four quarters. In Spanish language, she received three A's and a B throughout the year.

The children had varied rates of attendance. Ana, Lucho, Juan, and Luisa had very good attendance (98%, 98%, 96%, and 94%), while Susana had poor attendance (85%). Susana's absences were due to serious family difficulties (a house fire and a car accident).

Summary

Table 3 on pages 64 and 65 presents a summary of the data gathered for each of these five cases. In some ways, these children had

Table 3
Children Who Were "On Their Way" to Success in School

Child's name	Language at home	Language at school	English proficiency	Literacy at home	Family's attention to school	Literacy at school	English literacy	Spanish literacy	Attitude toward school	Attend-ance	Other factors
Ana	Spanish	English and Spanish	Moderate	Daily shared and self-initiated reading and writing	Frequently visited school; monitored homework daily	Highly systematic with daily opportunities for extended reading and writing	Slightly below grade level	On grade level	Excellent attitude and behavior	98%	By third grade, had attended three schools
Juan	Spanish	English and Spanish	Moderate	Daily shared and self-initiated reading and writing	Frequently visited school; monitored homework daily	Highly systematic with daily opportunities for extended reading and writing	Below grade level	Slightly below grade level	Excellent attitude but was sometimes too social in class	96%	By third grade, had attended three schools
Lucho	Spanish	English and Spanish	Moderate-Fluent	Occasional shared reading and writing; frequent self-initiated reading and writing	Frequently visited school; sometimes monitored homework	Highly systematic with daily opportunities for extended reading and writing	Slightly below grade level	On grade level	Good attitude but frequent disruptive behavior	95%	Had resided in U.S. for fewer than 1½ years

(continued)

Table 3
Children Who Were "On Their Way" to Success in School (continued)

Child's name	Language at home	Language at school	English proficiency	Literacy at home	Family's attention to school	Literacy at school	English literacy	Spanish literacy	Attitude toward school	Attend-ance	Other factors
Luisa	Spanish	Primarily English; some Spanish	Moderate	Occasional shared reading and writing; frequent self-initiated reading and writing	Rarely attended school events; sometimes monitored homework	Highly systematic with daily opportunities for extended reading and writing	Below grade level	On grade level	Good behavior; inconsistent reports of attitude	93%	Had resided in U.S. for fewer than 1½ years
Susana	Spanish	Primarily English; some Spanish	Moderate	Daily shared and self-initiated reading and writing	Frequently visited school; monitored homework daily	Highly systematic with daily opportunities for extended reading and writing	Slightly below grade level	On grade level	Good attitude, but somewhat inattentive in class	85% (due to fire and car accident)	Had resided in mainland U.S. for less than 1 year

profiles much like those of the highly successful students discussed in Chapter 3. They each engaged in frequent (though not always daily) family literacy interactions and they each had at least one parent who attended closely to their school activities. They were interested in and motivated toward school and learning, although in three cases there was some inconsistency in the level of interest and motivation. In their transitional bilingual education classrooms, they were receiving intensive instruction in Spanish and gradually increasing instruction in English. This compared well to the effective instruction received by the children who were proficient English language speakers. The only consistent and substantial difference between the two sets of profiles was in the length of residency in the United States: Those in the moderately successful group had been in the country for a very short time or had had their length of stay in the United States interrupted by a return to their native country. The similarity in their home and school profiles and their good rate of academic progress after such a brief period in U.S. schools led us to predict that these students were on their way to success and that a follow-up assessment in another year would likely find them identified as successful students.

CHAPTER 5

Children Who Struggled in School

Jacinto, a second grader, Octavio, a third grader, and David and Benito, both fifth graders, were judged to be experiencing significant academic difficulty. Beyond their history of school failure, these four children shared few characteristics. Although Octavio and David had resided in the United States for fewer than 3 years, Jacinto and Benito had been here for more than 7. Octavio was judged to have minimal English proficiency, Jacinto and David were described as moderately proficient, and Benito was described as proficient. In each case, their mothers described their own English proficiency as moderate. Mothers' schooling ranged from 7 to 12 years. What stands out about each of these cases is the multiplicity and complexity of the difficulties that they confronted almost daily. In order to fully understand the uniqueness of each of these cases, we have chosen to present each child's profile separately.

Jacinto

Jacinto was an 8-year-old boy who was in a general education second-grade classroom in a public school. He lived alone with his mother and had a 12-year-old sister who lived in Guatemala. His mother, Paola, had been in the United States for 7 years. She was enrolled in the Intergenerational Literacy Project and also attended English General Equivalency Diploma classes in the neighboring adult education center.

The portrait of Jacinto that emerged is one of general inconsistency. He was clearly a struggling reader and writer and not a consistently motivated learner, likely due to multiple reasons.

Jacinto's Language at Home and at School

Jacinto explained that he used English "at school, and (with) my cousins…and when I go to someone's house that talks English." His mother, Paola, also said that he spoke English with his friends and with the neighbors. She explained that Jacinto spoke Spanish to her because she did not understand English. Paola also reported that the reading she and Jacinto did together was mostly in English and that, at home, Jacinto wrote only in English. Paola stated clearly that she wanted her son to maintain the Spanish language and, at the same time, to acquire English. She said that when they read together, she took the opportunity to teach him both languages:

Hay algunas palabritas a veces que yo no entiendo, y me sirve [buscarla] en mi diccionario de inglés-español, la pongo aparte y le sirve a él también, [porque] él no sabe la traducción. Cuando está hablando en inglés, él no me puede traducir que es lo que dice en español. Yo quiero que él aprenda a traducir en español. Hay niños acá que sólo lo dicen en inglés, pero no en español, no saben que quiere decir la palabra. Entonces yo, a Jacinto, le estoy enseñando el significado en español. Ahorita sólo inglés le he estado enseñando porque como se va para el tercer grado es un poquito más avanzado.

There are some words that I don't understand, and so I gain something, I look them up in the Spanish-English dictionary, I put it aside, and that helps him as well, [because] he doesn't know the translation. When he is speaking in English, he can't translate what he is saying in Spanish. I want him to learn how to translate in Spanish. There are children that only know words in English, not in Spanish; they don't know how to say a word in Spanish. So, I teach Jacinto the meaning in Spanish. Right now, I have been working on English only, because he's going into the third grade and that's a little advanced.

With respect to Jacinto's use of language at school, and particularly his development of English proficiency, Jacinto's second-grade teacher, Ms. Harris, commented that Jacinto's sentences were not "clear and smooth." She also said that frequently his oral communication was "very choppy with like a verb left out." She added that "he gets his point across, but it's not smooth."

Jacinto's language knowledge may have been uneven and perhaps not developed sufficiently in either Spanish or English. In school, his placement in a general education classroom from the start allowed him no support for continued development of his first language. He also did not receive any supplemental support for development of English language skills in school.

Jacinto's Literacy at Home

Jacinto and his mother, Paola, read and wrote together often, although the regularity or routineness of these interactions is unclear. At the time of enrollment in the Intergenerational Literacy Project, Paola reported reading children's books, cookbooks, newspapers, and magazines, all in both English and Spanish. Among the writing activities she did at home, she included writing letters to her family, notes to Jacinto's teacher, and shopping lists. She also reported sharing stories with her son on a daily basis. Paola explained,

Siempre hemos compartido y estudiado, y siempre lo he ayudado con sus tareas. Hay madres que no le leen a sus hijos, yo siempre he sido muy cuidadosa en ese respecto.	*We have always shared and studied together, and I have always helped him with his homework. There are mothers who don't read to their children, I have always been quite careful with respect to this.*

Paola elaborated by providing specific examples. For instance, she said that they wrote letters to her daughter in Guatemala. She also said that

El escribe y hace cositas, dibujos, carteles con sus amigos, todo lo que son caricaturas…. Hizo un cartel en donde dice que él tiene tantos años y que tiene una hermana de tantos años, que él no tiene hermanos. También dice que le gusta la escuela para estar con sus compañeritos y jugar y salir al parque, también que su programa	*He writes and he does little things, drawing, posters with his friends, everything that is like a caricature …. He made a poster that said how old he is, that he has a sister that is so many years old, that he has no brothers. It also said that he liked school because he could be with his friends, and he liked to play, and go to the park, also that*

favorito es Power Rangers, y sus colores favoritos, los colores de Power Rangers. Muy bonito lo que hizo.

his favorite show is Power Rangers, *and that his favorite colors are the colors of Power Rangers. Quite nice what he did.*

During his interview, Jacinto said that he read at home and named two books that he read recently: *Ugly Duckling* and *Power Rangers.* He explained that he read with his mother and by himself and did so in both languages.

At the end of the literacy project, Paola took her literacy logs home with her, so they were not available for our review. As a result, we had no other evidence of literacy routines at home.

Jacinto's Family's Attention to School

In some ways, Jacinto's mother was very attentive to school and literacy learning. Contact between her and Ms. Harris, Jacinto's second-grade teacher, seemed to happen almost daily, when Paola picked up Jacinto from school:

Yo siempre estoy pendiente de él, y siempre le pregunto a la maestra [cómo se comporta], tu sabes que la maestra sabe cómo se comporta en la escuela. Yo sé cómo se comporta en la casa pero usted ya sabe que a veces se comportan diferente.

I'm always attentive and I always ask the teacher (how he behaves), you know, the teacher knows how he behaves in school. I know how he behaves at home, but you know they sometimes behave differently.

The regularity of parent-teacher interaction was apparent in Ms. Harris's comment: "I tell her all the time…he could be doing better."

Paola also responded to his teacher's requests for support by initiating a 30-minute home reading program.

Digamos que conmigo se pone a leer, entonces después lo dejo a él que lea solo. Pero siempre estoy con él, porque de lo contrario, él no agarrra solo un libro y se pone a leer. Se pone a leer (y) después se pone a ver la televisión. Entonces mejor…estoy con él y leemos los libros, los terminamos y cogemos

Let's say that he starts reading with me, and then I let him read by himself. But I'm always with him, because if not, he doesn't get a book by himself and read it. He starts reading and then starts watching TV. So better… I'm with him, and we read books and we finish them and then we

otros. También le hago spelling test, *start other ones. I also give him* le hago palabras para que él me las *spelling tests, I give words so* conteste. Hemos tratado de estudiar *that he answers me. We have* porque la maestra me suplicó de *tried to study because the teacher* que el niño está bien, pero que trate *pleaded with me, that the child* de ayudarlo. Yo sé que media hora *is doing well, but to try to help* no es nada para el porvenir de él. *him.... I know that half an hour* Me pongo a ayudarlo porque yo *is nothing for his future. I help* también no tengo nada que hacer *him also because I don't have* en la mañana, así que le dedico un *anything to do in the morning,* poco de tiempo a mi hijo. *so I dedicate some time to my son.*

Jacinto's inconsistent and rather sporadic improvements in the classroom led Ms. Harris to wonder whether there was also a pattern of sporadic and inconsistent support at home. She noted, for example, that "98% of the time, I never get his homework." On his report card, on the criterion "Completes and returns homework," Jacinto received an I (inconsistent) during the first quarter, an N (no, remains a weakness) during the second and third quarters, and an I during the fourth quarter.

Although Paola's concern for Jacinto's general well-being was evident to Ms. Harris, she seemed to be unaware of the extent of Paola's academic support and wondered whether Jacinto's mother was sufficiently involved in his school learning. She said, "She's very caring...it just—it seems, not to make a judgment, but it does seem as though schoolwork is not a number one priority."

Despite this comment, Ms. Harris also noted that when she informed Paola of her son's inconsistencies, Paola's immediate actions seemed to have an impact on Jacinto's behavior and performance:

If he hasn't been finishing his work and I'll complain to the mother about the inconsistencies, [that] he's not finishing his work, [that] he can do a lot better than what he does, for a week or so he will do better, and then, he'll kind of slip back and then it falls and he slips back slowly for another week or 2, and then I have him after school and then the mother comes in and then for 2 weeks it's good for a week and then it's kind of slow.

These data provide some evidence that Paola may have neglected some factors that relate strongly to success in school, such as homework completion and regular attendance.

Jacinto's Attitude Toward School

When asked what he liked about school, Jacinto said that he enjoyed being with his friends. His interest in school as a social activity was confirmed by Ms. Harris, who viewed Jacinto as being comfortable in the classroom environment:

> He's very social, he's very social. He fits in very well. He knows exactly what's going on in the room. He gets along great with the other children. They all like him…no matter what table he sits at. He's fine; he has no problems…and he's confident in himself. I think, you know, it's not like a lack of confidence.

Despite his apparent social confidence, academically, Jacinto was described as being dependent on others for task completion:

> He…relies heavily on others…even when we go to do an assignment he's always relying on whoever is sitting beside him, and it really doesn't… some of the children sort of know who does well in the class…. It doesn't really matter the ability of this person.

Ms. Harris also spoke of Jacinto's need for clear, explicit directions and expectations. She said, "[In order to pay attention and work well] he needs like specific instructions and he needs to know that you're firm."

Ms. Harris commented that Jacinto is "easily distracted" by others and not particularly motivated to learn, but rather focused on other activities:

> He's not highly motivated as far as curiosity. He very rarely raises his hand and answers a question if we're doing anything. If he writes stories, for example, he's always mentioning he can't wait to go to the store to buy more toys. He can't wait to go home to play with his toys.

> At the beginning of the year, he was off to a slow start, and then he sort of picked up…he's very inconsistent. He can have a good week where he'll get everything completed and finished, and then he has a week that…he just can't seem to focus.

At the time of the second interview, Jacinto had shown some overall improvement: "I think his attitude toward school is better, but it still could be a lot better." She added that "He volunteers…He'll raise his hand whereas he had never volunteered, volunteered to read, volunteered to say anything." However, Ms. Harris, was not confident that the change would last.

Paola was aware that her son's behavior could be considered erratic. She said,

Como le vuelvo a repetir, como cualquier niño, tiene a veces sus momentos que habla y que a veces no escucha a la maestra…. Sólo lo hacía de vez en cuando. La maestra, a veces, lo dejaba castigado. Lo hizo como cuatro veces. Yo le llamé la atención, lo castigué, y le dije que no me gustaba que estuviera así. La maestra lo cambiaba de asiento, porque él decía que otro niño le hablaba. La maestra desde que lo cambió, parece que allí le fue mejor a él.

As I said before, like any other child, he has some moments of talking with others, and sometimes he doesn't listen to what the teacher says. He only did that sometimes. The teacher, at times, would punish him. She did that around four times. I called this to his attention, I punished him, and told him that I didn't like him to behave in such a way. The teacher would change his seat in the class, because he used to say that another child would speak to him. Since the teacher changed his seat, it seems that he did better.

Jacinto's Literacy at School

We know little about the quality of Jacinto's first-grade school year because his teacher left the school system and did not participate in the study. We are reasonably sure, however, that during second grade he was offered good literacy instruction. Ms. Harris, his second-grade teacher, was highly respected by administrators and colleagues as a fine teacher who was particularly dedicated to teaching literacy. The researcher's field notes described a highly literate classroom where children had many opportunities to read and write. Literacy instruction in Jacinto's second grade consisted of an 80-minute daily instructional block led by Ms. Harris and Ms. Carmelo, the Title I reading teacher. Ms. Harris described how flexible grouping was used routinely during the literacy block:

During that time, using the trade books or the anthology we have a story for the week. We, together as a whole group, we introduce the story to the class, we do the vocabulary, we set the purpose for reading. Actually, a lot of times, we may partner read just to model the lesson because some of them are kind of, some of them are poor readers, some of them are actually reading, and then after that we do our flexible group. One day a week the children will read silently, the children that are able to read silently will read the stories silently while with work with a small group of children that possibly would find it difficult to read like that, and then we will come back together, discuss what we've read and this would probably be the end of the lesson. And then, you know, there are some days that they have to read again. We come together as a group, we discuss, we review the vocabulary, we may story map a story…again, we basically come together as a group. We split up for individualized instruction, small-group instruction, and then we come back together to discuss what we've done.

Ms. Harris also reported that students participated in extensive journal writing, both at home and at school, wrote and "published" their own books, and engaged in daily sustained silent reading.

Jacinto struggled in reading and writing in both first and second grades. While in first grade, two special progress reports were sent home. On January 13, his teacher informed the parent that Jacinto "lacks all basic skills" in reading. On March 29, the teacher wrote that "in math, reading, spelling, the child is showing poor performance on tests, inattention in class and difficulty with these subjects." She also noted that "Jacinto's reading has improved, however, he is still below grade level. More improvement is necessary if Jacinto is to go on to Grade 2." On his final report card, his grades indicated that he had made improvements in making predictions and in understanding what he read. Nevertheless, he was still struggling with sound-symbol correspondence.

Jacinto's difficulty in reading and writing continued in second grade. Ms. Harris said the following:

He's not really comfortable with it (reading). His writing…hasn't progressed like it should because…he writes whatever he has to write to get it done quickly. He's one of the first to finish. We went over the stories the other day, for example, and I think he was the only one in the room still…let me take that back; I have a couple of…real at risk…and this is not Jacinto, but the only one that should have been able to…(put) periods at the end of the sentence and carrying on it was just one…sentence.

In describing Jacinto's literacy progress, Ms. Harris again referred to his motivation and behavior.

He works well if you're sitting there with him and he's able to do the work and he seems to understand fine, but the minute you leave he's the one that's always fooling around or he's picking the book up or they're laughing and he doesn't stay focused very long.

The interviewer followed up with a specific question, and Ms. Harris elaborated:

Interviewer: He doesn't apply what you know he understands?

Ms. Harris: Right, and if I do get angry with him, if I'm very stern or I'll say, "You should be putting periods in," you know, "Now go back and reread this," he will do that.

By the end of the year, Jacinto was still struggling. When asked about Jacinto's reading level, his teacher said, "Well, we all read on the second grade, in the second-grade book, but and I would say in, in that book it's, it's poor. I'd say like a D, maybe a D."

She added, however, that there had been some change in his attitude toward reading. He was showing more interest and even taking books home:

But actually another positive thing, I'm trying to think back, is he's been asking to take books home…you know, where…he really didn't care whether he took a book home or not. But not on a regular basis, but more than he did…he sees a book of interest, he'll ask to take it home.

By the end of the year, Jacinto was still unable to read at grade level. On his report card, throughout the first three quarters, he received Ns (no, remains a weakness) in all reading behaviors, with the exception of summarizing, on which he received an I (inconsistent) each quarter. In the fourth quarter, he improved slightly, and was judged as "Making steady progress" on the behaviors "participates actively" and "applies reading to other subjects." He received only one N on "organizes and retells information" and was given I's in the remaining behaviors, which included the ability to use a variety of strategies to decode and understand text, and to summarize, elaborate, and clarify reading materials. In addition, he was judged as unable to write a coherent story or to punctuate and capitalize properly.

Jacinto's mother was aware of his struggle with reading. She said the following:

Lee demasiado lento y todavía no entiende muchas palabras, entonces ella, la maestra, me dijo que en tiempo de vacaciones yo le diera lectura. Hemos estado tratando de dar media hora de lectura ahora que está de vacaciones.	*He reads too slow, and he still doesn't understand many words, so she, the teacher, told me to read to him during vacation time. We have been trying to give half an hour of reading a day now that he has vacation.*

Jacinto's school attendance rate was quite low in both first grade (89%) and second grade (82%), which was perceived as a serious problem by his second-grade teacher. She said, "He's been absent 26 days this year so far and 90% of the time he doesn't bring a note." She commented that she thought that Paola's poor English skills might explain why she did not send notes to explain Jacinto's absences, but she was nonetheless concerned about not receiving an explanation. She said, "I know the mother isn't really comfortable with English but I told him you're supposed to bring a note even if they bring the note in Spanish." Ms. Harris reported that during the third and fourth quarters in school, Jacinto's absences decreased by half and he did begin to bring notes explaining his absences in English. It's also interesting to note that his mother's attendance at her own literacy classes was also sporadic.

Although Jacinto's first-grade teacher mentioned the possibility of retention, he was promoted to second grade and there is no record that he was recommended for special services.

In summary, the data in Jacinto's case suggest that his difficulty may have stemmed from a combination of factors: insufficient language development in both Spanish and English, apparent inconsistent attention to literacy and school learning at home, and inconsistent attendance in school causing gaps in both instruction and practice.

Octavio

Octavio was an 8-year-old child who was enrolled in a third-grade Spanish bilingual class. He was born in Puerto Rico and had been in the United States for 1 year, moving here when he was about to begin third grade. Octavio lived with his mother and father, a younger brother, Carlos, and his older sister, Susana, who was described in detail in Chapter 4.

As explained earlier, the year in which the study took place was a difficult one for Octavio's family. A few months after moving to the community, the family's apartment was destroyed by fire, and they subsequently moved to a housing project in the same neighborhood. The family was also involved in a car accident in which Octavio and his sister were injured.

Their mother, Esmeralda, enrolled in the Intergenerational Literacy Project in October 1994, 3 months after coming the United States. On entry to the project, she reported that she had attended school for 10 years in Puerto Rico and described her English proficiency as moderate. She reported that she hoped to learn "everything": to speak, understand, write, and read in English. Her literacy logs attest to her desire to develop literacy in English: After recording her entries in Spanish for the first month, she switched to writing in English.

Octavio's Language at Home and at School

According to Octavio, his mother, and his teacher, Mrs. Hernández, Spanish was his primary language at home and at school. He reported speaking only Spanish at home and at school, saying that he did not "know" English.

Mrs. Hernández's comments about Octavio's English language fluency were consistent with his self-assessment. She reported that the school's two Spanish bilingual third-grade classes were divided at the beginning of the year into high- and low–English-proficiency groups, with her students having less proficiency in English.

> I have all the students who didn't, who didn't perform in English. And the students who are coming from different, from different countries, um, that they just speak Spanish. So most of my classes are in Spanish. I'm doing ESL with them, but they are not a high ESL class.

Esmeralda understood that most of the instruction in Octavio's class was in Spanish, but she pointed out that he also was interested in the assignments he received in English.

Como él casi no sabe español, creo que no le están dando mucho inglés, pero a él también le gusta porque a veces lleva asignaciones en inglés

Since he hardly knows any Spanish, I think they are not giving him a lot of English, but he also likes it because some-

y él se ve bien interesado.	*times he has assignments in English and he looks very interested.*

On her literacy logs, approximately one third of the books Esmeralda reported reading to Octavio were in English, and she reported buying books for her children in English.

Octavio's Literacy at Home

At home, Octavio and his mother engaged in frequent literacy interactions. When reading in Spanish, they shared responsibility for reading aloud. When reading in English, Esmeralda read aloud to Octavio.

Octavio had struggled in his early years of schooling and was just beginning to learn to read in Spanish. For the first time, he was beginning to self-initiate reading at home. Esmeralda explained, "Él a veces lee también. Cuando Susana lleva los libros en español, él se sienta y los lee" (*"He reads sometimes, also. When Susana takes books in Spanish, he sits down and reads them"*). Esmeralda noted, however, that reading continued to be difficult for Octavio:

Pues en Octavio, pues que ha habido cambio, cómo te digo, que él ha aprendido a leer un poco más, pero que todavía como que se tranca ahí y lee así en sílabas.	*Well, in Octavio, well, that there has been change, how can I say, that he has learned to read more, but he is still like stuck there, and he reads like that, in syllables.*

During his interview, Octavio said that he read routinely, both in Puerto Rico and in his new home. He reported previously borrowing books from school. He said, "Yo leía en Puerto Rico unos cuentos que yo tenía, que la escuela me daba prestado, y después cuando se acababan las clases, yo los entregaba" (*"In Puerto Rico, I used to read some books that I had, that the school would lend me, and then when classes were over, I would return them"*).

Since moving to this country, Octavio said he read at home in both Spanish and English:

A veces, ella me lee libros que ella ha traído de la escuela donde ella estudia, en español y [e] inglés. Me lee y, y cuando ella no, cuando ella	*Sometimes she reads to me from what she's brought from the school where she studies, in Spanish and in English. She reads and,*

va a cocinar y no nos puede leer, pues yo lo leo.	*and when she doesn't, when she is going to cook and she can't read to us, well, I read them.*

His mother said that Octavio did not like to write at home, that he preferred to play. Octavio confirmed that he didn't write at home, but he indicated that it was because he lacked writing materials:

OCTAVIO: Algunas veces, en la casa vieja, yo escribía.	OCTAVIO: *Sometimes at the old house, I used to write.*
INTERVIEWER: ¿Por qué?	INTERVIEWER: *Why?*
OCTAVIO: Porque la escuela me había dado un bloque de papel. Pero como se mojó [en el fuego] todo no me lo pude llevar, y no puedo escribir, no tengo papel.	OCTAVIO: *Because the school gave me a pad of paper. But since everything got wet [in the fire], I couldn't bring it, and I can't write, I don't have paper.*

Octavio's Family's Attention to School

Octavio's mother was very involved in his education at school. She was aware that Octavio was having difficulty learning to read and kept frequent contact with Mrs. Hernández, Octavio's teacher.

Mrs. Hernández reported that Esmeralda was in the classroom "all the time" seeking strategies for helping Octavio. She noted, "She deserves credit for what he has accomplished—a team effort." At the end of the school year, Mrs. Hernández commented, "His mom has helped him a lot, too…. I feel that she has cooperated with Ms. García [Chapter 1 Spanish reading teacher] and I, um, a lot."

At home, Esmeralda supported Octavio's literacy development at school in several ways. As she reported upon enrolling in the literacy program, she asked about and helped her children with their homework on a daily basis. Most of the shared literacy events reported in her literacy logs were, in fact, school related:

Ayude [Ayudé] a mis niños con su tarea, vimos una pelicula del Bronx y me hicieron preguntas. (Era en inglés)	*I helped my children with their homework, we saw a movie of the Bronx and they asked me questions. (It was in English.)* [literacy log, 10/3/94]

Ayude [Ayudé] a Octavio con una tarea en español.   *I helped Octavio with homework in Spanish.* [literacy log,10/6/94]

I help my children with homework. [literacy log, 11/30/94]

I helped my children with homework social study [sic] and Spanish. [literacy log, 1/26/95]

I helped my children with the homework of math. [literacy log, 2/9/95]

Yesterday, we spoke of the activities in the school. Tomorrow they will have a party. [literacy log, 6/15/95]

The family's focus on the importance of homework was confirmed by Octavio, who explained that he did his homework as soon as he arrived home from school each day, frequently with his mother's support. He said, "Ella me ayuda, pero no me lo dice" (*"She helps me, but she doesn't tell me"*).

Beyond helping with homework, Esmeralda also spent additional time with Octavio on a daily basis as a result of Mrs. Hernández's suggestion. Esmeralda said, "La maestra me dijo que en mi casa lo ayudara a escribir, lo ayudara a leer, y ella se sienta con él y le da una ayuda en el salón" (*"The teacher told me to help him write at home, help him read, and she sits with him and helps him in class"*).

Despite Esmeralda's involvement with Octavio at home, Mrs. Hernández noted that "writing stories at home [is] too challenging for the level of home support that is available." In addition, his teacher stated that, despite Esmeralda's support for Octavio during the school year, she was not confident that she would work with him as consistently over the summer. Indeed, Esmeralda's literacy log entries in July indicated no reading with her children.

Octavio's Attitude Toward School

Mrs. Hernández noted that Octavio "wants to learn, [is] motivated, [has] good attendance, likes school and [is] pleased to do homework." At the end of the school year, Mrs. Hernández reported that Octavio's motivation had persisted: "He has, he had worked very, very, very hard because he was very, very, very behind [laugh] in the beginning of the year.... Octavio is very motivated to learn."

Octavio's mother also reported that he was a motivated learner, although she noted that he was previously unhappy in his school in Puerto Rico:

A él le gusta la escuela...pero, este, aquí yo lo veo como más entusiasmado que en Puerto Rico, porque en Puerto Rico él no se quería levantar, él lloraba al ir a la escuela y aquí no. Y aquí, yo lo veo que a él le gusta y la maestra, que él está bien, como que él se ve bien interesado y me gusta que él esté así.	*He likes school...but, um, here I see him more enthusiastic than in Puerto Rico, because in Puerto Rico he did not want to get up. He cried when he went to school, but not here.... I see that he likes it and the teacher—that he appears to be very interested and I like it when he is like this.*

Octavio's own comments confirm his mother's and his teacher's reports. He easily articulated classroom routines and described reading and writing as his favorite activities in school.

Octavio's Literacy at School

Octavio's school experiences were marked by considerable difficulty. Based on information recorded on his report card, his second-grade year in Puerto Rico was characterized by satisfactory work habits but little academic success. He received Cs, Ds, and Fs in all subjects.

In describing Octavio's classroom literacy program in third grade, Mrs. Hernández explained that her entire class that year was low in reading at the beginning of the school year and so she had modified instruction to meet their needs:

At the beginning of the year, the 90% of my class couldn't read. They couldn't read. Just few students read, read at the first-grade level. So, the other ones start to read in my classroom. At the beginning of the year, when I, I, I've noticed, I noticed that their need was reading and writing, they couldn't write, because they couldn't read, so they started to write, they didn't, they didn't use capital letters, punctuation, anything. Just few words and they didn't know about the sense of, a sense. So I started from there, and I made, we made, Cathy García and I, she's a Chapter 1 reading, Spanish reading. We made a commitment to help those students out. So we divided them, by Chapter 1 students. And I kept the other group, the rest of the group...now, they are in the writing process. Because we couldn't do that before, just one step at a time because it was very difficult for this group. This group, because they have no information, they had no skills, almost, no skills.

Mrs. Hernández explained that on a typical day, both groups of students spent a good deal of time reading in Spanish. Octavio, too, at several points during his interview, commented on reading in his classroom. He first explained, "Me pongo mis bultos, me quito el jacket y cojo un libro a [para] leer" (*"I put down my bags, take off my jacket, and get a book to read"*). Later in the interview, he described the context for reading: "Como no hay tantos libros de lo mismos, cogemos diferentes libros a [para] leer. A veces leemos [en] pareja cuando son los mismo libros, después escribimos a [en] pareja" (*"Since there are not enough of the same type of books, we take different books to read. Sometimes we read in pairs when they're the same books, we read the same stories in pairs, then we write in pairs"*).

He also described the reading and writing tasks: "Leemos lo que pasa en el cuento, escribimos lo que pasa en el cuento, el resultado, qué sitio era, en qué tiempo lo hicieron, qué pasó en el problema, la solución, todo eso" (*"We read about what happens in the story, we write about what happens in the story, the result, where it took place, when it took place, what happened with the problem, the solution, all that"*).

Both his mother and his teachers described Octavio as far behind his peers in literacy development. Octavio's mother believed that his instruction in Puerto Rico the previous year at least partially explained the difficulty he experienced in third grade.

ESMERALDA: Lo que pasa es que él, este, en Puerto Rico no le enseñaron lo suficiente a él, porque él ya está en el tercer grado, y él no lee como él debe leer y no escribe como debe de escribir.

ESMERALDA: *What happens is that he, in Puerto Rico they did not teach him enough because he is now in the third grade and he does not read how he should and he does not write how he should write.*

INTERVIEWER: ¿A qué te refieres con lo de que no lee como debe de leer y no escribe como debe de escribir?

INTERVIEWER: *What do you mean when you say that he doesn't read how he should read and he doesn't write how he should write?*

ESMERALDA: Porque él lee en sílabas.

ESMERALDA: *Because he reads in syllables.*

Mrs. Hernández also reported that at the beginning of the year, he was "not able to read or write at all" and "did not know the alphabet." During the third-grade year, he received supplemental instruction in a Chapter 1 Spanish reading class. Both Mrs. Hernández and Mrs. García, the Spanish reading teacher, suspected that Octavio's slow progress might have been due to a learning disability. To investigate this possibility they referred Octavio to the Child Study Team, the first step in the system for identifying students for special education services. In April, Mrs. Hernández reported that Octavio was reading at a second-grade level in Spanish. By the end of the school year, she reported that he had improved in reading and writing but was still far below grade level. She recommended that he continue in Chapter 1 reading and that he participate in the school system's summer literacy camp. No further reference was made to the special education referral process. Mrs. Hernández said the following:

> You can tell that he has improved a lot because at the beginning he couldn't, he couldn't read, he couldn't say anything, he couldn't write anything, and now he's writing, and he's writing the letters, the words, because he was just writing syllables, and now he's writing, um, words, so he has improved.

Later in the interview she returned to his level of performance and to the progress he had made: "He is, he's reading at the second-grade level, yeah. And at the beginning he couldn't even read." Octavio's report-card grades reflect the difficulty he was experiencing in reading and writing. In all areas relating to written language, he received marks indicating that he was weak or making inconsistent progress. In reading, his only clear progress was in the area of active participation. In speaking and listening, Octavio received the grade of P (progressing) for his participation in discussions and clear expression of ideas. For work habits and conduct, Octavio was rated I (inconsistent).

Octavio missed only 2 days of second grade in Puerto Rico and was absent 13 days during third grade. Most of those absences were attributed to the family's temporary homelessness after the fire in their home and the car accident in which both Octavio and his sister were injured.

In summary, the evidence suggested that Octavio had strong and consistent support at home, many opportunities to engage in literacy events with his mother and sister, effective and intensive instruction in school (at least during his third-grade year), support for development of both Spanish and English language and literacy, and good school attendance. Octavio's difficulty in literacy learning was not explained by the role his family played, his language difference, or the effectiveness of the classroom instructional program. Rather, in Octavio's case, it is likely that a full diagnostic assessment by the Child Study Team would have been beneficial in explaining his difficulty in learning to read and write.

David

David was a 10-year-old child attending a fifth-grade bilingual class in a public school. He had experienced a good deal of transience, beginning his schooling in Puerto Rico, spending a year in Philadelphia, Pennsylvania, returning to Puerto Rico, and coming to the community where the study took place just a year earlier. A year after returning to the United States, David's parents divorced. Since his return to the United States, he had been very unhappy and, at the time of the study, was seeing a therapist. David's mother, Laura, enrolled in the Intergenerational Literacy Project in November of his fifth-grade year.

David's Language at Home and at School

David's fourth-grade teacher recalled that he was "clearly Spanish dominant." It seems, however, that David learned English quickly. His mother expressed amazement at his rapid acquisition of oral English skills, and his fifth-grade teacher also said that his production and comprehension of English were quite good. In fact, David's interview was conducted in English. When asked when he spoke Spanish, he replied, "Mostly all the time I speak English, but I don't know that much." His mother reported that, "El más escribe en español, y lee en español, pero habla más en inglés" (*"For the most part, he writes in Spanish and he reads in Spanish, but he speaks more English"*).

David's Literacy at Home

David's mother Laura was particularly dedicated to supporting her son and his school success. Both she and David reported that she enrolled in the ILP as a birthday present to her son. There is ample evidence that, after her enrollment in the project, she and David routinely engaged in shared literacy. Their descriptions suggest that their literacy interactions were sometimes purposefully intended to support David's schoolwork, while at other times they were initiated for the purpose of getting things done during the routine of their daily lives

Upon entry to the ILP, Laura reported reading a variety of books, including self-help psychology books, parenting books, and children's books, and newspapers, letters from her family, bills, and school information. She also reported frequent writing activities, such as letters, notes to her sons, shopping lists, and filling out welfare forms. Laura also kept a diary. In the daily entries of Laura's literacy log, she reported frequent uses of literacy throughout her day and week. Her entries suggested that both she and David used literacy in ways that were purposeful and meaningful and that they initiated literacy to "get things done" during the routine of their daily lives.

Le ayude [ayudé] hayer [ayer] a llenar unas tarjetas postales de San Valentin [Valentín] que le va a entregar a sus maestros y compañeros de clase. (literacy log, 2/12/95)	*Yesterday, I helped him write cards for Valentine's Day that he will give his teachers and classmates.*
Lei [Leí] hayer [ayer] con David las tarjetas que le dieron sus compañeros de clase por el dia [día] de San Valentin [Valentín]. (literacy log, 2/16/95)	*Yesterday I read some cards with David that his classmates gave him for Valentine's Day.*
Estube [Estuve] ayer leyendo con David un recibo de telefono [teléfono] le estaba esplicando [explicando] sobre unas llamadas extras que tenia [tenía] y lei [leí] una carta que me llego [llegó] de Haucin [Austin]. [literacy log, 3/28/95]	*Yesterday I was reading the phone bill with David. I was explaining to him about some extra calls I had made, and I read a letter I got from Austin.*
David me escribio [escribió] una nota y cuando llegue [llegué] de la escuela la vi. Hiba [Iba] para casa de su papa [papá]. [literacy log 4/19/95]	*David wrote me a note and when I came back from school I saw it. He was going to his father's.*

Similar evidence of routine literacy use appeared in interview data. Laura reported the following:

Siempre él me deja una nota porque yo le dejo una nota a él. Le digo: "David, estoy en tal sitio, vengo más o menos a tal hora; Dios te acompañe o te quiero mucho." Entonces él me deja una nota a mí …que dice: "Mami, me fui con papi, I love you o bendición." Siempre me deja una nota.

He [David] always leaves me a note because I always leave him a note. I tell him, "David, I'm at such and such a place. I'll be back at such and such time. God bless or Love ya lots." Then he always leaves me a note saying, "Mommy, I went with Dad, I love you or God bless." He always leaves me a note.

On entry to the literacy project, Laura reported never going to the library. After joining the project, she obtained a library card and, in an entry in her literacy log, she reported reading a book with David that she borrowed from the library. David stated that he asked his mother to bring books in English home from the project's library. Laura's literacy project teacher reported that during visits to the project library and class visits to the public library, Laura often requested help in choosing books to take home to David. Laura emphasized that David wanted books in English.

Although David reported without elaboration that his mother read to him at home, Laura's project teacher remembered quite clearly the first time Laura took a book to read to David. The book, she explained, was in a plastic bag with a notebook for illustrating or writing about the book. Laura returned to school the next day saying how much they both enjoyed reading the book and commented that she would do this more often.

In David and Laura's case, storybook reading events also provided an occasion for intergenerational learning, as described by David in this dialogue during his interview:

Interviewer: Do you ever read when you are at home?

David: Read? My mom reads me books.

Interviewer: Your mom brings you books? Is that what you said?

David: Yeah.

Interviewer: Oh, where does she bring the books from?

David:	From the English class.
Interviewer:	Really? Do you like to read with your mom?
David:	Yup. I teach her.
Interviewer:	You teach her? Tell me about that.
David:	To talk English.
Interviewer:	Tell me about that. Give me an example. When did you have to teach her?
David:	I tell her to don't talk Spanish, to talk English.
Interviewer:	So she can practice?
David:	Yup.
Interviewer:	So what kinds of things do you do when you're reading a book together?
David:	She has to read it to me. I don't read it for her 'cause she's not practicing. So she reads it to me.

In addition, it seems that Laura routinely tried to influence David's reading behaviors by modeling for him her own interest in reading. The following dialogue from Laura's interview provided one example:

LAURA: Desde que yo estoy aquí [the Intergenerational Literacy Project], tú sabes, me he interesado más en que él lea..., hay veces yo le digo, "voy a leer," y él me dice, "tú y tu lectura," porque me paso diciéndole que voy a leer a ver si se le meto en la cabeza.

LAURA: *Since I started coming here [the Intergenerational Literacy Project], you know, I've become more interested in his reading...sometimes I tell him, "I'm going to read," and he says, "you and your reading," because I'm always telling him that I'm going to read so he'll get the idea in his head.*

INTERVIEWER: ...pero lees o lo dices no más.

INTERVIEWER: *...but do you read or do you just say it?*

LAURA: Yo, yo me paso leyendo todo el tiempo. Yo leo mucho, entonces yo le digo a él: "voy a leer" siempre. Antes yo no le decía que iba a leer, pero ahora le digo, "D, voy a leer un

LAURA: *I'm always reading. I read a lot, so I tell him, "I'm going to read." Before I never told him I was going to read, but now I tell him, "D, I'm going to read for*

rato," y él me dice, "tú y tu lectura." (laughs)	*a while." And he says to me, "You and your reading." (laughs)*
INTERVIEWER: Y le has comprado libros?	INTERVIEWER: *Have your bought him books?*
LAURA: El tiene libros y yo voy a la biblioteca y busco libros, pero antes yo no hacía eso. Ahora pues hice membrecía y, tú sabes, y trato de que él se…	LAURA: *He has books and I do go to the library to look for books but before I didn't do that. Now, I became a member and you know, I try to get him to…*
INTERVIEWER: Y él va a la biblioteca?	INTERVIEWER: *And does he go to the library?*
LAURA: Sí.	LAURA: *Yes.*

There was good evidence that Laura's personal literacy behaviors changed after her entry into the literacy project and that the change in behavior influenced her literacy interactions with David.

David's Family's Attention to School

During David's fourth- and fifth-grade school years, patterns of parent-teacher interactions changed significantly. His fourth-grade teacher, Ms. Verona, recalled that "both parents were super involved and just interested in how he was doing, on an ongoing basis, not just parent conferences." Ms. Verona noted that toward the end of the year, David's father stopped coming to school and that David's mother, Laura, spoke to her about it. Laura reported this same information to her literacy project teachers. This was around the same time that David's parents separated and later divorced.

During the first interview in April of the academic year, Mr. Krashen, David's fifth-grade teacher, reported having had only one meeting with David's mother. The limited parent-teacher interaction was confirmed by Laura on her literacy project intake form, completed in December of David's fifth-grade year, where she reported that she "rarely" contacted her child's teacher.

Data indicate, however, that although the frequent visits to the classroom stopped, David's mother paid attention to school in other ways. Laura reported asking David daily about his experiences at school. As an example, she shared the following information: "Me dice…a veces me ha dado quejas de que lo regañan mucho. Yo le digo por qué lo regañan.

Me dice [que es] porque él se entretiene mucho" (*"He says...sometimes he complains that they scold him too much. I tell him, why do they scold you? He says [it's] because he fools around too much"*).

After a meeting requested by David's teacher, Laura reported,

Yo hablé con el maestro y el maestro me dijo que él se…que a él le gusta mucho hablar con el que está al lado, con unos amigos. Y este, yo hablé con D, estábamos hablando los tres, y él [el maestro] me dijo que él se entretenía mucho.	*I talked to his teacher and his teacher told me that he...he likes to talk with his neighbor, whoever sits beside him, with friends. And well, I spoke with David, the three of us were talking, and he [the teacher] said he fools around too much.*

Following this meeting with the teacher and David, Laura reported that "Yo le pregunto todos los días cómo se portó" (*"Every day, I ask him how he behaved"*). Laura's awareness of and interest in monitoring David's school responsibilities was also evident in a discussion about homework:

En la casa no hace tarea. No le dan tarea, y si le dan, es de vez en cuando. La hace en el salón…. El dice que le dan tarea y que él la deja hecha en el salón, pero la vez que yo fui a ver al maestro no me dijo nada, y a mí se me olvidó preguntarle. Fíjate, yo tengo que saber, porque el año pasado no le daban tarea.	*At home, he doesn't do homework. They don't give him homework, and if they do, it's only once in a while. He finishes it all in school…. He says they give him homework and he finishes it at school, but once when I went to see the teacher, he didn't say anything, and I forgot to ask him. I need to know because last year, they didn't give him homework.*

David also talked about not having homework, but he said, when he did, his mother helped him:

David: Homework that we had to read a book, she read it to me.

Interviewer: So she would help you with your homework?

David: Yup.

Interviewer: Does she help you with your homework now?

David: No, no. But I don't get homework.

David's Attitude Toward School

David's fourth-grade teacher described him as a "normal fourth grader" who "felt pretty good about the classroom...about being here and socially that helped him make friends and work with his buddies." In fact, she said, "He was really doing great." Her approach to individual children may account for the successful experience David had in her classroom:

> I always try to do, I mean not just last year, but always just to make it really homey for them. Just really where they can come and just relax and enjoy what they're doing while they are here. Specifically, after I learned how many kids are you know [in a] really bad environment. Not just a bad environment, but just unstable and just a lot of family problems and things like that.

According to his teacher, Mr. Krashen, David's attitude toward school changed dramatically in fifth grade. In the initial interview, Mr. Krashen cited David's behavior as his greatest difficulty in school. His mother confirmed that Mr. Krashen had called her a few times to discuss David's behavior in class. During a meeting with Mr. Krashen, Laura explained that David thought that he had been singled out as a troublemaker and and that he was living up to expectations. Mr. Krashen was responsive to this conversation and said that perhaps he had been "a bit hard" on David. Following that meeting, David and Mr. Krashen's relationship improved. In the final interview, Mr. Krashen reported a dramatic change in David's attitude. He described him as more motivated, positive, and productive.

David's mother Laura reported that David did not enjoy school as much as he did in Puerto Rico. She said that "it is a struggle to get him out of bed in the morning." She attributed this change to an overall unhappiness he had felt since leaving Puerto Rico. In fact, she commented in her interview that on various occasions, he threatened to injure himself to convince her to take him back:

El lo estuvo extrañando tanto que ya me tenía a mí mal. Pero que ya desde que lo llevé al terapista [terapeuta], ya está mejor. Porque él decía cosas terribles, como decía, "Yo me voy a tirar por la escalera."

He was missing it so, so much that it was driving me crazy. But since I took him to the therapist, he's been better. He used to say terrible things, things like, "I'm going to throw

No, una vez, me dijo, al principio que se iba a tirar por la ventana, y yo vivía en un tercer piso. Porque si él se tiraba por la ventana, se rompía una pierna y yo le cogía pena y lo llevaba a Puerto Rico.

myself from the top of the stairs." No, one time, he told me first that he was going to jump out the window, and I lived on the third floor. Because if he jumped out the window, he would break a leg and I would feel bad for him, so I would take him back to Puerto Rico.

Laura reported that when they were in Philadelphia, David's school experience was the worst. She also mentioned that despite the fact that he had adapted socially, he still had not adjusted to the school. She seemed to believe that the academic schedule at least somewhat explained David's recent difficulty. She said that David was very energetic and in Puerto Rico he could go outside at midday and get exercise. Here, she said, he could not do the same things. David, himself, reported enjoying nonacademic subjects (music, art, gym) and disliking math.

David's Literacy at School

Unlike the students identified as attaining high or moderate academic success, neither David's fourth- or fifth-grade teachers were noted for teaching effectiveness. Interview data indicated that his recent literacy instruction lacked both direction and intensity in Spanish and English.

His literacy instruction in fifth grade was marked by few systematic routines. Mr. Krashen described a typical literacy lesson in his fifth-grade classroom in this way:

Well, I use, you know, a pad and easel because the blackboards here are very hard to write on so I find that I write big, you know, and I have markers. What I've been trying to do is I've tried to in some way hit on the different genres and I've tried to get them accustomed to different types of literature, different areas where they might be interested. We've worked a lot on realistic fiction because I figure that might be a place, kind of a grounded place, kind of a little bit more reality…. We did a lot with Judy Blume this year at the beginning of the year and we…did a lot with kind of taking the stories apart and see how they were put together, what are events in the story, how the story ends up. I really try

91

to break it down.... I have 8 or 10 different ways of doing story maps and story progression, but I just felt that sometimes one fits in better with a certain student.

In response to a question about Spanish reading, Mr. Krashen explained,

Yeah, I do the Spanish reading with them but the Spanish reading by the time we're in fifth-grade level, I wouldn't call it every day. I would say we might do some literature in Spanish maybe two or three times a week.

David, too, was asked to talk about what he reads in school:

Interviewer: What kinds of things do you read?

David: He reads to us.

Interviewer: Oh, really? What kinds of stuff does he read?

David: Umm, what's the name again? umm... *The Indian in the Cupboard. The Indian in the Cupboard.*

Interviewer: And do you like it?

David: Yup.

Interviewer: And so he reads it aloud to you all while you listen?

David: Yup.

Interviewer: And what do you do after that?

David: (no answer)

Interviewer: Do you do anything...talk about the story?

David: Sometimes we talk about the story, sometimes we play after...sometimes we write about it.

Interviewer: And do you ever sit down and read a book by yourself in class?

David: Umm, we don't got a lot of books so we have to share.

Interviewer: You have to share. So do you sit with a friend?

David: Sometimes.

Interviewer: And what do you do after you read with your friends or when you read by yourself?

David:	We work or play.
Interviewer:	And do you ever have to write a story or a letter or a report or anything like that?
David:	We did that a long time ago, too.
Interviewer:	Oh, you did that? What type of things did you do?
David:	We wrote a lot of stories.
Interviewer:	What kinds of stories do you like to write?
David:	Umm, the one like I told you.
Interviewer:	The one of the *Indian in the Cupboard*? OK, so, you don't have to do any kind of writing now, at the end of school?
David:	Umm [shaking his head no].

In response to questions about David's literacy performance, Mr. Krashen described David as a struggling reader. He said, "His English speaking and his listening comprehension...are fine. It's the reading and writing...which I think has been neglected." In the final interview, Mr. Krashen again stated that David "can read but gets very frustrated" and that he is "afraid to write."

David, himself, offered some interesting comments about his performance in reading and writing:

Interviewer:	And do you ever have to read in Spanish or write in Spanish?
David:	I *could* write in Spanish.
Interviewer:	And do you read and write in English too?
David:	I don't know how to write.
Interviewer:	You don't know how to write, but do you read in English?
David:	I know how to read a little bit.

David's mother was aware of her son's struggle with reading and writing in school, but she was unable to explain why he was not reading or writing better:

INTERVIEWER: Algo más que quieras decirme sobre el uso del lenguaje de David, sobre la escuela, o sobre sus usos de la escritura o lectura en la casa?

INTERVIEWER: *Is there something else you want to tell me about David's use of language, about school, or about his use of writing and reading at home?*

LAURA: Que a él le gusta, él tiene los libros y los papeles por allí listos pa(ra) algo, pero como que todavía no se ha preparado, no sé.

LAURA: *That he likes, he likes to try new things, but he has books and papers all ready for something, but it's as if he's not quite ready yet. I don't know.*

David's report-card grades were satisfactory, although his grades declined during his fifth-grade year. In fourth grade, he earned a consistent B average. In fifth grade, he averaged Cs, but with a high degree of inconsistency. At the beginning of the year, he received Ds, improving gradually each quarter until the final period when he earned a B average. It is difficult to know whether the grade changes indicate a change in performance or a difference in the standards adhered to by the fourth- and fifth-grade teachers. There were no written comments on any of David's report cards.

David had moderate school attendance in fourth grade, missing 16 days of school and had poor attendance in fifth grade when he missed 26 days. He was not recommended for retention either of the 2 years, nor was he recommended for any services for children with special learning needs.

In summary, David's elementary school experiences seem to have been complicated by several factors. It is likely that his transience, his parents' divorce, his inconsistent interest in and motivation toward school and learning, and the apparent inconsistency in the quality of his instructional opportunities at school all contributed to lower academic achievement.

Benito

Benito was a 10-year-old boy attending a general education fifth-grade classroom in a Catholic school. He had one sibling, an older brother in the eleventh grade. His mother, Daniela, was enrolled in the ILP and also was taking ESL classes. She was originally from Guatemala, where she completed her secondary education.

Benito's Language at Home and at School

Benito reported that he spoke English at school and Spanish at home. In assessing his English skills, his teacher said that although he had some verb tense problems (for example, overusing the present tense in past-tense situations), he "speaks English pretty well." His mother, Daniela, confirmed that he spoke Spanish at home, but also said that he spoke English with his brother, friends, cousins, and neighbors, and that he also spoke some English with his father. Daniela said that Benito was fluent in both languages and that she was responsible for his maintaining his Spanish, "pero sí habla bien los dos idiomas porque de eso sí yo me he encargado de que no se olvide de su lenguaje porque es mejor para él" (*"but he does speak well both languages because I have made sure that he doesn't forget his language because it's better for him"*). She added that she also taught him how to read and write in Spanish: "El sabe leer en español porque yo le enseño" (*"He knows how to read in Spanish because I teach him"*).

In his interview, Benito confirmed what his mother reported about his reading and writing in Spanish:

> I read a little in Spanish…. My mother taught me how to read in Spanish, and I could write it too, but only when sometimes…she tells me to…I write…easy stuff…. My mother tells me to write…words…in Spanish…just to practice.

Benito's Literacy at Home

When she first entered the literacy project, Daniela reported that she and her husband both enjoyed reading, and at that time identified some of her favorite authors, including Gabriel García Márquez and Miguel de Cervantes. She also reported reading newspapers and magazines in both English and Spanish.

Daniela and Benito read and wrote together and they both reported reading books from the ILP and from the public library. In his interview, Benito recalled that when he was younger, his mother read to him passages from the Bible: "The stories of the Bible my mother read to me when I was about 6." He also reported that he and his mom went to the library together and his mother "rents books."

They used literacy to accomplish practical purposes, particularly writing birthday cards and letters to relatives in Guatemala, "porque

cuando son los cumpleaños de mi familia, yo le digo vamos y hace-
mos una postal, y [la escribimos en] español porque no entienden inglés" (*"because when it's any family member's birthday, I tell him,
let's go and we write a postcard, and we write it in Spanish because
they don't understand English"*).

Daniela also actively taught Benito Spanish reading and writing.
She left notes for him, and Benito took messages for her:

Cuando me dice "Mami, cómo se escribe tal palabra," entonces la escribo o tengo un pizarracito [pizarrita o pizarroncito] allí… cerca del refrigerador y entonces se la digo…se escribe así o a veces…cuando yo voy a salir y él está afuera y no quiere entrar, entonces le dejo una nota allí, "me fui a…," "voy a regresar a…," o "voy a la tienda" o cualquier cosa. A veces los tíos le llaman por teléfono y dan los números de teléfono en español también.	*When he tells me "Mommy, how do you write such word," I write it for him or I have a little blackboard there…near the refrigerator and I tell him…you write it like this…or sometimes when I'm going to go out and he is outside and he doesn't want to come in, then I leave him a note there "I went to…," "I am coming back at…," or "I went to the store," or anything. Sometimes his uncles and aunts call and they dictate phone numbers in Spanish as well.*

Despite Daniela's practice of involving Benito in literacy events,
he appeared not to like reading or writing and engaged in extended literacy activities only when he was made to do so. Benito explained,
"I'm OK at reading…but reading I just do in the classroom."

Daniela was concerned about Benito's lack of self-initiated literacy activities, reporting that he preferred to play outside or with computer games. She explained that although Benito sometimes read com-
ic books, magazines, and the Bible, she usually had to force him to
read something:

Cuando vengo del trabajo, yo le pregunto qué ha hecho todo el día, me dice "ver televisión, jugar." Entonces yo le digo "OK." Le doy un libro pequeño y le digo, "lee algo." Le gusta leer la ciencia ficción.	*When I come back from work, I ask him what he's done the whole day, he says, "Watch television, play." Then I tell him, "OK." I give him a small book and tell him to "read something." He likes to read science fiction.*

She blamed herself for his lack of motivation and disinterest in reading:

Pero yo sé que no le he inculcado el hábito de la lectura porque no le gusta. No le gusta ni por más que yo intento y a mí sí me encanta leer. Yo leo bastante de noche, incluso leo más que ver televisión, pero a mis hijos no les gusta y a mi esposo también le gusta leer, pero a ellos no les gusta. Yo no sé a qué se deba, pero yo pienso que de chiquititos si yo…les hubiera leído cuentos de noche, yo pienso que sí les hubiera acogido el hábito de la lectura, pero el problema acá es de que uno no tiene tiempo.	*But I know that I have not instilled the habit of reading because he doesn't like it. He doesn't like it no matter what I do, and I do love reading. I read a lot at night, I even read more than I watch television, but my sons don't like it and my husband also likes reading, but they don't like it. I don't know what it's due to, but I think that if I had read to them at night when they were little, I think that if I had instilled the habit of reading, but the problem here is that one doesn't have any free time.*

Daniela also reported that Benito rarely wrote at home except for homework or when he misbehaved:

Escribe nada más que…el home-work que le dejan, de allí no le gusta escribir. A veces cuando él hace algo malo, yo le digo "vaya a su cuarto y me tiene que escribir tal parte, tal parte, tal parte." Entonces enojado y bien disgustado lo hace, pero lo hace. Tiene bonita letra. Yo no sé cómo tiene bonita letra si no escribe mucho.	*He writes only…the homework that he has, he doesn't like to write. Sometimes, when he misbehaves, I tell him, "Go to your room and you have to write this part, this part, this part." So, mad and very angry he does it, but he does it. He has nice handwriting. I don't know how his handwriting is so nice, if he doesn't write much.*

When asked about writing at home, Benito recalled only rare instances when he wrote for a particular purpose: "Once I did [write]. I sent a letter to this baseball player and he gave me an autograph."

Daniela's literacy log entries provide no supporting evidence of her attempts to read and write with Benito. She used the log as a daily journal, recording her own activities and her thoughts about the literacy class; there was no mention of home activities.

Benito's Family's Attention to School

There is ample evidence that Benito's family paid attention to and was involved in his schoolwork. Daniela, for example, monitored his homework and took him to the library when he needed to do research for a book report or a class project and she participated actively in such projects. She said, "Yo le acompañaba a la biblioteca y vamos [e ibamos] a traer libros y escogíamos que proyecto era el mejor para hacer. Se inventó como un radio…y unos cables que le daban luz" (*"I would go to the library and we would get books and we would choose what project would be better to do. He invented like a radio…with some cables that light"*).

Daniela, however, believed that her limited English proficiency did not allow her to help him as much as she would like:

Cuando él va a la escuela y le dejan…deberes de matemáticas… de inglés que tiene que buscar palabras en el diccionario…y este proyecto de ciencias, en eso sí le ayudo, pero en lo demás no le puedo ayudar mucho…él sabe más inglés que yo. Entonces no le puedo ayudar gran cosa. Es más, él me ayuda a mí.	*When he goes to school and he has…math homework…English, when he has to look up words in the dictionary…and this science project, in that I do help him, but in the rest I can't help him too much…he knows more English than I do. So my help is no big deal. On the contrary, he helps me.*

She also said that although she is often unable to help, Benito's father and older brother sometimes provide help:

Cuando él estaba en kinder y primer grado y segundo grado, yo le ayudaba porque era más fácil para mí. Pero ahora ya no le puedo ayudar. A veces le ayudo en matemáticas que todavía me acuerdo de algunas cosas, le ayudo, pero de lo contrario él le pregunta a mi hijo mayor o a mi esposo que ellos sí saben inglés.	*When he was in kinder[garten] and first grade and second grade, I would help him because it was easier for me. But now, I can't help him. Sometimes I help him in math because I still remember of some things, I help him but if not, he asks my older son or my husband who do know English.*

Benito's teachers confirmed his parents' involvement in his academic work. His fourth-grade teacher recalled that during that year, his parents, and especially his father, spoke to Benito several times about his school behavior and performance. After these talks, she said, Benito's work did improve. Unfortunately, his progress was not steady. Daniela also remembered that during his fourth-grade year, she worried that he would fail, that she would tell him that he was going to have to repeat the grade. She said, "Ya en los últimos meses cogió pena y entonces sí estudiaba y ya subieron sus notas, y así fue como ganó…sesenta y setentas, como decir una C" (*"In the last months he started to feel ashamed and so he did study and his grades got better, and that is how he got sixties and seventies, like a C"*).

Daniela tried to motivate her son and described how she provided positive reinforcement when he demonstrated some expertise:

El dice que no le gusta la escuela… cuando él sabe algunas cosas más que yo, le digo "ya vio, ya vio mi hijo, si usted no va a la escuela usted no sabe leer y no sabe lo que sabe." Porque a veces sí le gusta cuando yo no sé algo y él me lo explica se siente feliz porque él sabe más que yo así en inglés. Yo le digo, "Ya vio esta es la ventaja de que usted vaya a la escuela y usted esté aprendiendo todo."

He says that he doesn't like school…when he knows something more than I, I tell him, "You see, you see my son, if you did not go to school, you would not know how to read, and you would not know what you know." Because sometimes, he does like it when I don't know something and he has to explain to it me. He feels happy because he knows something more than I in English. I tell him, "You see, that is the advantage of going to school and that you are learning everything."

Benito's parents met with his teachers primarily at the teachers' request. Daniela explained, "En El Sagrado Corazón cuando entregan los report cards tenemos por fuerza que ir y hablamos con la maestra. Entonces ella nos dice los problemas del niño" (*"In Sacred Heart when they hand in report cards we are forced to go and talk to the teacher. So then, she can tell us about the child's problems"*).

The fourth-grade teacher also called Daniela three other times to meet with her. Ms. Robillard recalled that both parents attended the requested meetings. She described Benito's parents as "super nice" and explained that it was during these meetings that Benito's father would talk to him.

During his fifth-grade year, Daniela attended school meetings by herself, and the language difference between her and Benito's fifth-grade teacher, Sister Joan, apparently presented a substantial barrier to effective communication. Sister Joan explained that, aside from the required report-card meetings, she had only one additional contact with Daniela. She reported that the meeting was initiated by Benito's parents who

> wrote a note asking if could they come up…I thought they would both come up to see the fifth-grade teachers…so that we could explain, but we couldn't really do much explaining to her because she couldn't understand us.

In a previous interview, Sister Joan referred to the same meeting:

> But she came up one day as I said at the beginning of the year and…she spoke hardly no English and…Sister and I were both getting after him because…he is so lazy, he wasn't doing a thing and the mother just stood there and smiled and because she didn't understand what we were saying, which is sad you know.

Benito's Attitude Toward School

The fourth-grade teacher described Benito as a "capable student who just didn't study." His fifth-grade teacher described him as likeable and courteous, but lazy. Her overall impression was that Benito was a child who "could do better…has potential," but lacks motivation. She further explained, "and I don't think he hates learning, but…he's the type [who]…won't do any more than you make him." She did note that "most of the time" he completed his homework. Benito was very clear about his attitude toward school. He said that he was bored at school and did not like any subject except science. His disinterest and lack of motivation were evident in his tone and in his words:

> Sometimes…I get to school late. When I'm in school, I don't like it. I don't like it all 'cause I'm tired. 'Cause I always go to sleep late. I get bored in school; there is nothing to do.

Asked why he went late to school and why he went to sleep late he said, "Sometimes I wake up late, and sometimes I don't want to get dressed quick. I just look at stuff outside."

His mother, Daniela, was very aware of the problems her son had at school and of his attitude toward school. When asked how Benito was doing at school, she corroborated comments made by his teacher: "Como decimos nosotros…no muy bien. El ha tenido problemas en todos los grados porque es muy arrogante. El es inteligente, pero no le gusta estudiar. Especialmente en cuarto grado tuvo muchos problemas" (*"As we say…not very well. He has had problems in all grades because he is so arrogant. He is intelligent, but he doesn't like to study. Especially in fourth grade, he had so many problems"*).

At the end of the school year, Sister Joan did not "perceive any noticeable changes" in Benito's overall academic performance or attitude toward school. She again stressed that he could do better if he were more motivated. She said, "I think he should be able to do average work if he pushed himself…. I don't see the motivation there, you know, and I think he's babied perhaps. He's immature." During this interview, she also spoke briefly about his school history and made a reference to a conversation she had with his kindergarten teacher:

> I was talking to Sister Clara, teaching third grade now, but she felt that in, I don't know if I told you this or not before, but she felt that in kindergarten, he should have repeated because he was so immature then. I meant to look up his age…to see what age he was when he started.

Evidence from all sources confirms that Benito had a history of low motivation and poor attitude toward school. It did not seem to be related to a particular teacher, nor was it accepted or ignored by his parents.

Benito's Literacy at School

Benito's academic profile showed an overall poor performance. A review of his cumulative record revealed that as early as his kindergarten year, he was perceived to be a struggling student. In Grade 4, he was well below average, earning mostly Ds and Fs. By the end of the year, he had improved to an average of a C-. His fifth-grade report card showed a pattern of Cs and Ds. He was described as reading "in the bottom fourth of his class." Evidence of Benito's low performance in reading also was found in the researcher's field notes: "She [Sister

Joan, his fifth-grade teacher] showed me his recent reading unit test—he fell below the acceptable score on almost half the items."

Only Benito's fifth-grade teacher, Sister Joan, was available to be interviewed. In describing his writing, Sister Joan explained that his handwriting was messy, but that she "thought he did pretty well on...the paragraph this morning he started on." His teacher generally attributed his difficulty not to his ability or specific knowledge, but to his poor effort and motivation. Sister Joan said that she had never seen Benito read a book during free time or self-initiate writing. However, the interviewer's field notes read,

> I looked around when I asked if Benito read books on his own. The room was very bare with one bookshelf that looked like it had old books. She only mentioned that he read the books connected with the social studies curriculum.

Sister Joan described her classroom literacy activities as based mostly from a fourth- and fifth-grade text and the accompanying workbooks and worksheets. She explained that most of the time, a selection took a week to complete. As a prereading activity, she explained that she engaged her class in vocabulary activities, provided a summary of the story, and talked about the author. Children read the story silently and then reread it as a class. After reading the story twice, Sister Joan asked questions to check their comprehension and the students completed the workbook pages that accompanied the lesson. On the basis of these comments and her observations of the classroom environment while in the school and classrooms, the interviewer concluded that instruction was generally quite traditional. Teachers seemed to follow a textbook model of having children read the text and respond to comprehension questions. There was little indication that students worked in small groups or that they received individual support. Classrooms libraries were limited to old textbooks and a few worn trade books. Writing instruction seemed to be focused primarily on form and mechanics.

Benito had fine school attendance during his fifth-grade year (97%) and had not been retained in any grade. There was no recommendation for any type of supplemental or special services.

As in the cases of the other low-performing students, Benito's profile is unique. Data suggested relatively frequent, though likely not daily, practice of family literacy, explicit awareness by both mother and child of the intergenerational benefit of parent-child literacy interactions, and consistent and responsive monitoring of school behavior and performance. In school, there was some indication that Benito's literacy learning opportunities were largely limited to traditional, school-based literacy activities. Beyond textbooks, classrooms had few reading materials and classrooms generally were not "print-rich." Despite recognition that Benito was experiencing difficulty as early as kindergarten, there was no evidence that he ever received any supplemental instruction or support.

Looking Across the Cases of Struggling Students

As indicated in Table 4 on pages 104 and 105, in each of these four cases there were unique and special circumstances that contributed to the children's learning difficulties. At the start of the chapter, we noted that what stood out in these cases was the multiplicity and complexity of the factors that complicated their learning lives. Among the difficulties experienced by at least one of the children was transience in both living and schooling, family difficulties including divorce and drug abuse, learning disability, low motivation toward school and learning, inconsistent opportunities at school to learn and practice reading and writing, and insufficient opportunities to fully develop proficiency in both Spanish and English.

Even so, with the exception of Octavio, whose learning difficulty may have been primarily explained by the presence of a learning disability, there were also some clear differences between these children's home and school learning experiences and those of their more successful peers. Missing from these children's learning profiles were four particular qualities that were present in the profiles of their higher achieving peers: (1) Despite generally supportive home contexts, none of the children experienced the day-in and day-out, year-in and year-out, consistency of parental attention to academic success that was evident in the cases of their more successful peers; (2) while some teachers were particularly attentive to home-school connections and some parents were similarly attentive to such connections, no child experienced the continuity of either explicit or implicit collaboration between parents and teachers that was evident in the cases of their

Table 4
Children Who Struggled in School

Child's name	Language at home	Language at school	English proficiency	Literacy at home	Family's attention to school	Literacy at school	English literacy	Spanish literacy	Attitude toward school	Attendance	Other factors
Jacinto	Spanish and English	English	Moderate—Fluent	Occasional shared and self-initiated reading and writing	Frequently visited school; did not monitor homework	Highly systematic with daily opportunities for extended reading and writing	Below grade level	Unknown	Poor attitude and disruptive behavior in school	82%	Experienced learning difficulty from the start of schooling
Octavio	Spanish	Spanish with daily English as a Second Language period	Minimal	Daily shared reading and writing; had just begun to self-initiate reading	Frequently visited school; monitored homework daily	Highly systematic with daily opportunities for extended reading and writing	Below grade level	Below grade level	Excellent attitude and behavior	93% (absences due to fire and car accident)	Had resided in mainland U.S. for less than one one year; recommended for Special Education evaluation

Table 4
Children Who Struggled in School (continued)

Child's name	Language at home	Language at school	English proficiency	Literacy at home	Family's attention to school	Literacy at school	English literacy	Spanish literacy	Attitude toward school	Attendance	Other factors
David	Spanish and English	Primarily English; some Spanish	Fluent	Daily shared and self-initiated reading and writing	Rarely attended school events; monitored homework daily	Unsystematic with limited opportunities for extended reading and writing	Below grade level	Unknown	Poor attitude; labeled behavior problem by teacher	86%	By fourth grade, had attended four schools; family life marked by divorce and drug abuse
Benito	Spanish and English	English	Fluent	Occasional shared reading and writing; never self-initiated reading or writing	Attended formal school events; monitored homework daily	Highly systematic; limited opportunities for extended reading and writing	Below grade level	Unknown	Poor attitude and good school behavior	97%	Experienced learning difficulty from the start of schooling

more successful peers; (3) no child experienced the continuous, high-quality, school instruction that was evident in the cases of their more successful peers; (4) no child brought to the learning context a consistently high level of motivation to learn.

Given the complexity and uniqueness of the individual profiles, we are, of course, unable to draw firm conclusions about the influence of the absence of these characteristics on their academic experiences. We believe it is reasonable to say, however, that the consistent absence of each of these factors from the profiles of three of the four struggling learners suggests that they may at least partially account for the children's negative school experience.

CHAPTER 6

Lessons Learned

In the years since we began working in this urban community, we have had many conversations with teachers about the children they teach and their success or failure in school. Often, as the discussion turns to the role parents play in their children's learning, we hear comments such as the following:

> Parents have similar, if not more, difficulties in reading and writing and really have minimal involvement with their children's performance.
>
> Some parents are involved, but most of the parents are not involved because of the language barrier.

As we examined the literacy experiences of the 12 children in this study, it was clear to us that, for the parents of these children, these impressions were simply not valid. Contrary to commonly held beliefs, we did not find that parents' proficiency in English, years of education, or personal literacy skills played an important role in their ability to support their children's academic success. We did not find parents who were not involved, not interested, or not dedicated to their children's learning. We also did not find instances of either success or failure that could be explained solely by the types of events that occurred either at home or at school. Instead, we came to understand that, for these children, success in school was a complex process, dependent on both the actions of parents and teachers separately, and perhaps most importantly, on their interactions. Children who succeeded had parents and teachers who took actions that were, either by design or by accident, both complementary and consistent. In this chapter we articulate the lessons we learned from studying the actions of the children, parents, and teachers participating in this project.

Lesson 1: Immigrant Parents' Ability to Support Their Children's Academic Success

In the families of the children we studied, parents varied widely in their years of formal education (from 5 to 12), in their years in the United States (from 1 to 20), in their levels of English proficiency (from minimal to moderate), and in their own literacy abilities (from nonreader to proficient reader in Spanish). Like Auerbach (1995b), we found no patterns in the data to suggest that any of these factors correlated with parents' interest in or ability to support their children's school learning. Instead, we found that in every case, the practice of family literacy was an important and integral part of family life long before parents joined the Intergenerational Literacy Project. In every family, parents and children reported spending some time in literacy interactions prior to their enrollment in the literacy project. Some parents did tell us, however, that their participation in the Intergenerational Literacy Project influenced the consistency and frequency with which they shared literacy with their children and, in many cases, the particular ways in which they engaged their children before, during, and after storybook reading.

In addition to the general finding that all parents engaged in some shared literacy activities, we also learned that there were important characteristics in the family literacy experiences of the children who were identified as having high or moderate success. In these cases, the literacy interactions were frequent, most often daily, and varied. Children and parents read and wrote together and alone and used literacy for a wide range of purposes. They were explicitly involved in supporting each other's learning. The awareness that parent and child were engaged in reciprocal teaching and intergenerational learning seemed to bring special importance and joy to the literacy event.

In addition to engaging in literacy for the purposes of shared learning, however, literacy also occurred for many other purposes. Children engaged in literacy for play, parents and children read and wrote during the course of their daily lives, and parents and children read and wrote for both pleasure and enjoyment. In other words, as Taylor and Dorsey-Gaines (1988) reported in one of the first studies of family literacy, shared literacy interactions were not always for the purposes of "practicing" reading and writing; rather, they were often simply woven into the fabric of everyday life, occurring so adults and children might accomplish routine goals and responsibilities.

Lesson 2: Ways Parents Exercise Their Roles

Although not all parents attended school meetings and functions, they all paid careful attention to their children's school activities. In some cases, parents maintained a strong connection with their children's teachers, visiting and talking with them frequently. In others, parents rarely spoke with the teacher, but carefully monitored school performance by attending to homework and asking about school each day. Once again, parents differed not in the existence of interest or involvement, but rather in degree and consistency. Further, in cases in which parents were consistently and routinely involved, it was almost always because they, rather than the teacher, initiated the routine contact.

Our observations were not unlike those of Goldenberg (1987) who, in a study of low-income Hispanic parents' contributions to their first-grade children's reading success, found that all parents were capable of and willing to support their children's learning, but that the school made no systematic attempt to enlist their aid. As we considered these findings, we were reminded of a point made by Lareau (1989). In order to understand home-school relationships, she said, we need to understand home-school linkages. As we examined and re-examined our data, it was evident that in cases in which children were experiencing clear or moderate success, there were particular ways in which parents and teachers created linkages. For example, in some cases, walking children to and from school provided a routine context in which parents and teachers could share their concerns, comments, and ideas. In other cases, enlisting specific help from parents on particular types of homework assignments created routine and effective linkages.

It was in the ways that parents chose to exercise their roles and responsibilities that we also saw the influence of social and cultural capital as described earlier by Bourdieu (1973) and Lareau (1989). We found that in those cases in which parents shared the linguistic and social backgrounds of the teachers, they monitored their children's school learning by visiting with the teacher frequently, asking questions, and seeking clarification as necessary. In contrast, in cases in which teachers and parents differed both linguistically and culturally, parents were more likely to monitor their children at a distance from school, checking their homework, asking them questions, attending formal school meetings, but seldom initiating contact on their own or raising questions or topics not raised by the teacher.

We also discovered contexts that *did not* work in the development of linkages, that created a barrier to home-school relationships. Particularly, inviting Spanish-speaking parents to conferences and meetings with English-speaking teachers diminished several parents' contact with the school. Parents chose not to return, and sometimes teachers chose not to invite them when there were language differences.

Further, in a few cases, teachers complained that parents did not come to open house, PTO meetings, field trips, or other common school activities. This was seen as evidence of inadequate or inconsistent interest in their children's learning. This, too, is an observation that has been made by other researchers in earlier studies (for example, Chavkin, 1993; Delgado-Gaitan, 1990; Valdés, 1996). Yet as Comer (1986) noted, parents' lack of participation in such events often is related to an array of factors, including race, income, language, education, and past negative experiences with schools. He concluded that inviting parents to school is not enough; parents must be provided clear mechanisms for involvement.

Lesson 3: The Importance of Complementary Home and School Environments

In cases in which children were highly successful in school, they had both a high level of parental support and involvement in academic learning and effective and intensive instruction in literacy in school. In 1991, Snow and her colleagues provided compelling evidence that, although strong parental factors could compensate for weak schooling, even those children with nurturing home literacy environments did poorly in reading if school practices were inadequate. Throughout our study, we found that children's literacy learning opportunities at school varied widely. Teachers and children alike described a wide range of activities, some rich and effective in supporting children's literacy learning, others less so. In some cases, children seemed to have rich and consistent instruction during 1 of the 2 years, but inconsistent or ineffective instruction in the other. As one would expect, in every case in which children were experiencing clear or moderate success, opportunities to learn and practice literacy in either English or Spanish were described as systematic and reasonably intensive. Conversely, in three of the four cases in which children were struggling, classroom opportunities to learn and practice literacy in English, Spanish, or in both languages were judged to be limited during at least 1 of the 2 years. Like Snow and her colleagues, our data lead us to conclude that "excellent classrooms can compensate for less than ideal home conditions, but that ideal home conditions cannot always compensate for very poor classrooms" (p. 161).

Lesson 4: The Complexity of School Failure

In cases in which children experienced serious difficulty in school, their failure was not explained by the role their parents played in their academic learning. Instead, there were complex and varied reasons for their failure and few similarities in their profiles. The array of factors included relatively weak or inconsistent school instruction, inconsistent home support, transience, divorce, low motivation, and, in one case, a possible learning disability. In every case in which a child was failing, there was more than one obstacle to academic success.

Despite the high degree of complexity in these profiles of failure, however, we also found some commonalities, not in what was present within the individual profiles, but rather, in what was missing. In three of the four cases in which children were failing, they lacked consistent, daily routines for the practice of family literacy; continuity of either explicit or implicit collaboration between parents and teachers that leads to complementary home and school learning experiences; continuous, high-quality school instruction over more than 1 year; and a consistently high level of motivation to learn.

We concluded that to understand and help reverse school failure, we must understand individuals within the full context of their home and school lives. We must seek a complete understanding of the richness of all students' opportunities to learn to read, write, and speak in both English and their first language; of the ways their practice of family literacy and other family interactions complement their opportunities to learn in school; of the personal learning abilities and disabilities that may promote or inhibit learning; and of the ways schools provide or limit access to parents as they attempt to support their children's academic success.

This finding is of particular importance in relation to widespread views on parents' roles in children's success and failure. Moles (1993) reported that in a recent national survey of teachers, parents' lack of interest and support was the most frequently cited educational problem. Similarly, authors of a recent report on the role of the family in children's school success came to the "sobering conclusion that a large proportion of homes are not providing very high platforms for the schools to build on" (Barton & Coley, 1992, p. 42). As a result of such surveys and reports, family literacy is seen by many as the solution to the academic failure experienced by so many linguistic and cultural minority children. Valdés (1996) has suggested that such a focus represents "an attempt to find small solutions to big problems" (p. 31).

In sum, our evidence suggests that despite sometimes limited English proficiency, low levels of formal education, and few economic resources, when parents were provided opportunities to learn from and collaborate with their children's teachers, all of them were willing and able to do so, and most did so consistently and effectively. Yet, in a few cases, their children still failed. Our challenge as teachers is to look beyond family issues to find productive paths to success for Latino children who struggle.

What Should We Expect of Family Literacy?

Since the implementation of the Intergenerational Literacy Project, we have been asked countless times what effect the program is having on the school achievement of the children in the families who participate. We often have been told that if we wish to continue to secure funding for the project, we must be able to document that as a result of parent participation, children are "doing better" in school. Indeed, we, too, would like these children, and all children, to succeed in school. But, as we saw in the cases of Benito, David, Jacinto, and Octavio, looking to family literacy interventions as the primary solution to the problem of school failure for many Latino children is to dismiss the complexity of the challenges they face both inside and outside of school.

García (1994) reported that nonwhite and Hispanic students drop out of high school at two to three times the rate of white students. Solís (1995) noted that at least half of the Latinos who failed to complete high school never began attending, dropping out by the end of sixth grade.

Statistics related to Latino children who remain in school are equally troubling. Duany and Pittman (1990) reported that Latino youth were 2.5 times as likely as non-Hispanic whites to be two or more grades behind in school. Data from the National Assessment of Educational Progress (Mullis, Owens, & Phillips, 1990) indicated that the reading, math, and science skills of Latino 17-year-olds are roughly comparable to the skills of non-Hispanic white 13-year-olds. Further, evidence suggests that Latino children are less likely than their majority peers to have access to the same levels of resources and quality education. According to a 1989 report by the Children's Defense Fund, Latino children are attending segregated schools in increasing numbers and these schools are found to have qualitative differences from schools that serve non-Hispanic whites, including lower levels of teacher education and experience, lower amounts of actual instructional time and equipment, poorer facilities, lower per-student expenditures, and lower teacher expectations.

Outside of school, Latino children face challenges unmatched by many of their nonminority peers. According to a report of the National Center for Children in Poverty (1996), the rate of poverty among young Hispanic children is high (1.7 million children) and increasing more rapidly than among other racial and ethnic groups. Unless addressed in substantial ways, these rates are projected to more than double by the year 2026. Solís (1995) reported that Latino males work more hours while attending school than any other group and that they drop out of school for economic reasons. Further, their lack of English fluency and low levels of education often relegate them to minimum-wage jobs with little opportunity for advancement.

As we search for an answer to the problem of school failure for Latino children, it is tempting to look to the family as the source of the solution. Indeed, studies such as ours and others like it (Ada, 1988; Delgado-Gaitan, 1990; Quintero & Huerta-Macías, 1990; Shanahan, Mulhern, & Rodriguez-Brown, 1995) suggest that family literacy interventions have the potential to help children achieve academic success. However, as we celebrate these successes, we must not ignore the evidence that tells us that, although family literacy programs are important and may make important contributions to children's ultimate school success, they cannot and will not, by themselves, "correct" the problem of underachievement by Latino children. Relying on them to do so allows us to place the blame for school failure in the wrong place and to deny our societal responsibility to confront and correct the full range of issues that will help Latino and other children of color to succeed in U.S. schools and society.

Conversations With Teachers: Suggested Prompts

1. Describe the kinds of reading and writing activities in which your students participate on a typical day.

2. Tell me about _____'s participation in class during reading and writing activities.

> Expected topics:
> - Level of participation
> - Attitude
> - Success with tasks
> - Strengths
> - Needs
> - Reading and writing ability

3. In what ways does _____ use reading and writing on his or her own?

> Expected topics:
> - Pick up books on own
> - Talk about books
> - Share books with friends
> - Write notes or letters
> - Share writing with friends

4. Tell me about the role of _____'s family in his or her literacy learning.

5. Describe _____'s use of Spanish and English.

6. Tell me about your general impressions of _____'s interactions with his or her peers and with you.

7. How does this student's overall performance compare with the other students in your class?

8. Describe this student's attitude toward school and learning in comparison with the other students in your class.

Conversations With Parents: Suggested Prompts

1. You have participated in the Intergenerational Literacy Project for the past _____ months. Tell me about the types of reading and writing activities you and your child share.

2. What do you notice about your child's uses of literacy at home?
   Expected topics:
   - use of literacy during play
   - use of literacy "to get things done"
   - homework routines

3. What do you notice about your child's uses of language at home?

4. Tell me about your child in school.
   Expected topics:
   - conversations with child
   - likes and dislikes
   - successes and failures

Learner Intake Form

Language of interview: _____

INTERGENERATIONAL LITERACY PROJECT
LEARNER INTERVIEW

Date of interview: _____   Date of enrollment: _____199____

Interviewer: _____   Class assigned: _____

Name:_____   Phone number: _____

Address: _____   Country of origin:_____

Male ___ Female ___ White ___ Black ___ Latino ___ Asian ___ Other: ____

Age: 16-24 ___ 25-44 ___ 45-59 ___ 60+ ___

Children:

First Name	Last Name	Gender	Date of Birth	Grade	School	Teacher
_____	_____	____	_____	____	_____	_____
_____	_____	____	_____	____	_____	_____
_____	_____	____	_____	____	_____	_____
_____	_____	____	_____	____	_____	_____
_____	_____	____	_____	____	_____	_____
_____	_____	____	_____	____	_____	_____

Relationship to child(ren) _____

Will you bring any of your children with you to class? _____

(If yes, check the names of those who will accompany parent)

Willing to commit 2 hours per day, 2 days/evenings ___   3 days/evenings ___

4 days ___   per week

First Language: _____   Other Language(s): _____

In which language(s) do you read? _____

In which language(s) do you write? _____

How long have you lived in the U.S.? _____

How long have you lived in this town? _____

Do you work outside the home? _____   If yes, where? _____

What do you do at your job? _____

Have you ever worked outside the home? _____   What did you do? _____

_____

Do you receive public assistance? If so, what type?_____

Education:

Years of formal schooling in U.S.A. _____   Years of formal schooling in another country _____

High School Diploma or equivalent? _____   Prior ABE? _____   ESL? _____

Where? _____

How did you hear about this program?

What do you hope to learn in this program?

What do you read at home? (Include titles and languages)

books? _____

newspapers? _____

magazines? _____

mail? _____

children's homework? _____

school information? _____

other? _____

When you read, what do you do if you come to a word you can't read?

If you don't understand what you read, what do you do?

What do you do to help you remember what you read?

What are the characteristics of a good reader?

What do you write at home? (be specific/language)

letters? _____

notes? _____

shopping lists? _____

journal/diary? _____

other? _____

Is there anything else you would like to write?

What do you do if you can't spell a word?

What do you do to check your writing?

How do you know when something you've written is good?

How often do you:

	Daily	2-3x weekly	Once a week	Rarely	Never	N/A	Comments
go to the library?							
exchange books with others?							
buy books?							
share stories with your child(ren)?							
ask about your child(ren)'s homework?							
help with your child(ren)'s homework?							
write notes or messages to your child(ren)							
write to or meet with your child(ren)'s teacher?							

Approximately how many books are in your home? _____
Comments _____

_____

How often:

	0–2 hours	2–4 hours per day	4–6 hours day	6+ hours	Rarely	Never	N/A	Comments
do you view TV?								
do your children view TV?								
do you view TV together?								
do you discuss what you've viewed?								

English Proficiency: _____ none _____ minimal _____ moderate _____ proficient

Literacy Log

Name: _____

Month/Year: _____

Date	Reading, writing, viewing, and talking activities I shared with my child or children	Child's name and age
_____	_____	_____
_____	_____	_____
_____	_____	_____
_____	_____	_____
_____	_____	_____
_____	_____	_____
_____	_____	_____
_____	_____	_____
_____	_____	_____
_____	_____	_____
_____	_____	_____
_____	_____	_____
_____	_____	_____
_____	_____	_____
_____	_____	_____
_____	_____	_____
_____	_____	_____
_____	_____	_____
_____	_____	_____
_____	_____	_____
_____	_____	_____
_____	_____	_____
_____	_____	_____

Literacy Log

Name: _____

Month/Year: _____

Date	Reading, writing, viewing, and talking activities of personal interest
____	_____
____	_____
____	_____
____	_____
____	_____
____	_____
____	_____
____	_____
____	_____
____	_____
____	_____
____	_____
____	_____
____	_____
____	_____
____	_____
____	_____
____	_____
____	_____
____	_____
____	_____
____	_____

Conversations With Children: Suggested Prompts

1. Tell me about a typical day at school.

> Prompts:
> - Tell me about today at school.
> - Can you tell me more?
> - What part of the day did you like best?
> - What part of the day did you like least?

2. Tell me about reading and writing in school.

3. Tell me about what you do after school.

> Prompts:
> - What did you do yesterday?
> - Is that day typical?
> - Can you think of a day when you did something completely different? Can you tell me about that day?

4. Tell me about the ways you read and write at home.

> Prompts:
> - What did you read or write yesterday?
> - Was that typical?

5. Tell me what languages you speak?

> Prompts:
> - When do you speak Spanish?

• When do you speak English?

6. How was this year the same or different from last year?

7. What is different since your (mom or dad) joined the ILP?

Working Codes

1. Academic performance

2. Attitude toward reading and writing

3. Change in academic performance

4. Change in family literacy

5. Change in language proficiency

6. Change in literacy performance

7. Child's learning history

8. Classroom literacy

9. English language proficiency

10. Family comes to school

11. Family literacy

12. Change in family literacy

13. Family pays attention to school

14. Instructional context

15. Language choice

16. Learning strategies

17. Literacy performance

18. Motivation

19. Perceptions of literacy

20. School-initiated contact

21. Self-initiated literacy

References

Ada, A.F. (1988). The Pajaro Valley experience: Working with Spanish-speaking parents to develop children's reading and writing skills through the use of children's literature. In T. Skutnabb-Kangas & J. Cummins (Eds.), *Minority education: From shame to struggle* (pp. 223–238). Philadelphia, PA: Multilingual Matters.

Applebee, A., Langer, J., & Mullis, I. (1988). *Who reads best? Factors related to achievement in grades 3, 7, and 11. The nation's report card.* Princeton, NJ: National Assessment of Educational Progress.

Auerbach, E.R. (1989). Toward a social-cultural approach to family literacy. *Harvard Educational Review, 59,* 165–181.

Auerbach, E.R. (1995a). Deconstructing the discourse of strengths in family literacy. *Journal of Reading Behavior, 27,* 643–661.

Auerbach, E.R. (1995b). Which way for family literacy: Intervention or empowerment? In L.M. Morrow (Ed.), *Family literacy connections in schools and communities* (pp. 11–28). Newark, DE: International Reading Association.

Barton, P.E., & Coley, R.J. (1992). *America's smallest school: The family.* Princeton, NJ: Educational Testing Service.

Bogdan, R.C., & Biklen, S.K. (1992). *Qualitative research for education,* (2nd ed.). Boston, MA: Allyn & Bacon.

Bourdieu, P. (1973). Cultural reproduction and social reproduction. In R. Brown (Ed.), *Knowledge, education, and cultural change* (pp. 487–511). London: Tavistock.

Bourdieu, P. (1977). Cultural reproduction and social reproduction. In J. Karabel & A.N. Halsey (Eds.), *Power and ideology in education* (pp. 487–511). New York: Oxford University Press.

Bronfenbrenner, U. (1974). *Is early intervention effective? A report on longitudinal evaluations of preschool programs, Volume 2.* Washington, DC: Department of Health, Education, and Welfare.

Chavkin, N.F. (1993). Introduction: Families and the schools. In N.F. Chavkin (Ed.), *Families and schools in a pluralistic society* (pp. 1–20). Albany, NY: State University of New York Press.

Children's Defense Fund. (1989). *Testimony of the Children's Defense Fund before the Select Commitee on Children, Youth and Families.* Washington, DC: U.S. House of Representatives.

Cochran-Smith, M. (1983). Reading to children: A model for understanding texts. In B.B. Schieffelin & P. Gilmore (Eds.), *The acquisition of literacy: Ethnographic perspectives* (pp. 35–54). Norwood, NJ: Ablex.

Comer, J. (1986). Parent participation in the schools. *Phi Delta Kappan, 67,* 441–446.

Delgado-Gaitan, C. (1990). *Literacy for empowerment: The role of parents in children's education.* New York: Falmer Press.

Delgado-Gaitan, C. (1994). Sociocultural change through literacy: Toward the empowerment of families. In B.M. Ferdman, R.M. Weber, & A.G. Ramírez (Eds.), *Literacy across languages and cultures* (pp. 143–170). Albany, NY: State University of New York Press.

Delgado-Gaitan, C. (1996). *Protean literacy.* Washington, DC: Falmer Press.

Delpit, L. (1988). The silenced dialogue: Power and pedagogy in educating other people's children. *Harvard Educational Review, 58,* 280–298.

Duany, L., & Pittman, K. (1990). *Latino youths at a crossroads.* Washington, DC: Children's Defense Fund.

Durkin, D. (1966). *Children who read early: Two longitudinal studies.* New York: Teachers College Press.

Epstein, J. (1996). Perspectives and previews on research and policy for school, family, and community partnerships. In A. Booth & J.F. Dunn (Eds.), *Family-school links: How do they affect educational outcomes* (pp. 209–246). Mahwah, NJ: Erlbaum.

García, E. (1994). *Understanding and meeting the challenge of student cultural diversity.* Boston, MA: Houghton Mifflin.

Goldenberg, C.N. (1987). Low-income Hispanic parents' contributions to their first-grade children's word-recognition skills. *Anthropology and Education Quarterly, 18,* 149–179.

Heath, S.B. (1983). *Ways with words.* Cambridge, UK: Cambridge University Press.

Henderson, A., & Berla, N. (1994). *A new generation of evidence: The family is critical to student achievement.* Washington, DC: Center for Law and Education.

Kellaghan, T., Sloane, K., Alvarez, B., & Bloom, B. (1993). *The home environment and school learning: Promoting parental involvement in the education of children.* San Francisco, CA: Jossey-Bass.

Krol-Sinclair, B. (1996). Connecting home and school literacies: Immigrant parents with limited formal education as classroom storybook readers. In

D.J. Leu, C.K. Kinzer, & K.A. Hinchman (Eds.), *Literacies for the twenty-first century: Research and practice* (pp. 270–283). Chicago, IL: National Reading Conference.

Lareau, A. (1989). *Home advantage: Social class and parental intervention in elementary education*. New York: Falmer Press.

Miles, M.B., & Huberman, A.M. (1994). *Qualitative data analysis*. Thousand Oaks, CA: Sage Publications.

Mishler, E.G. (1986). *Research interviewing*. Cambridge, MA: Harvard University Press.

Moles, O.C. (1993). Collaboration between schools and disadvantaged parents: Obstacles and openings. In N.F. Chavkin (Ed.), *Families and schools in a pluralistic society* (pp. 21–53). Albany, NY: State University of New York Press.

Moll, L.C., & Greenberg, J.B. (1990). Creating zones of possibilities: Combining social contexts for instruction. In L.C. Moll (Ed.), *Vygotsky and education: Instructional implications and applications of sociohistorical psychology* (pp. 319–348). New York: Cambridge University Press.

Mullis, I.V.S., Owens, E.H., & Phillips, G.W. (1990). *Accelerating academic achievement: A summary of findings from 20 year of NAEPS*. Princeton, NJ: Educational Testing Service.

National Center for Children in Poverty. (1996). *One in four: America's youngest poor*. New York: Columbia School of Public Health.

Paratore, J.R. (1993). An intergenerational approach to literacy: Effects on the literacy learning of adults and on the practice of family literacy. In D.J. Leu & C.K. Kinzer (Eds.), *Examining central issues in literacy research, theory, and practice* (Forty-second Yearbook of the National Reading Conference, pp. 83–92). Chicago, IL: National Reading Conference.

Paratore, J.R. (1994). Parents and children sharing literacy. In D. Lancy (Ed.), *Emergent literacy: From research to practice* (pp. 193–216). New York: Praegar.

Paratore, J.R. (1995). Implementing an intergenerational literacy program: Lessons learned. In L.M. Morrow (Ed.), *Family literacy connections in schools and communities* (pp. 37–53). Newark, DE: International Reading Association.

Potts, M.W., & Paull, S. (1995). A comprehensive approach to family-focused services. In L.M. Morrow (Ed.), *Family literacy connections in schools and communities* (pp. 167–183). Newark, DE: International Reading Association.

Quintero, E., & Huerta-Macías, A. (1990). All in the family: Bilingualism and biliteracy. *The Reading Teacher, 44*, 306–312.

Quintero, E., & Velarde, M.C. (1990). Intergenerational literacy: A developmental, bilingual approach. *Young Children, 45*, 10–15.

Reading Excellence Act of 1998, H.R. 2614, 105th Cong., 2d Sess. (1998).

Seaman, D., Popp, B., & Darling, S. (1991). *Follow-up study of the impact of the Kenan Trust Model for family literacy*. Louisville, KY: National Center for Family Literacy.

Seidman, I.E. (1991). *Interviewing as qualitative research*. New York: Teachers College Press.

Shanahan, T., Mulhern, M., & Rodriguez-Brown, F. (1995). Project FLAME: Lessons learned from a family literacy program for linguistic minority families. *The Reading Teacher, 48,* 40–47.

Snow, C.E., Barnes, W.S., Chandler, J., Goodman, I.R., & Hemphill, L. (1991). *Unfulfilled expectations: Home and school influences on literacy*. Cambridge, MA: Harvard University Press.

Solís, J. (1995). The status of Latino children and youth: Challenges and prospects. In R.E. Zambrana (Ed.), *Understanding Latino families: Scholarship, policy, and practice* (pp. 62–81). Thousand Oaks, CA: Sage.

Sticht, T.G. (1992). The intergenerational transfer of cognitive skills. In T.G. Sticht, M.J. Beeler, & B.A. McDonald (Eds.), *The intergenerational transfer of cognitive skills: Volume 1: Programs, policy and research issues* (pp. 1–9). Norwood, NJ: Ablex.

Sticht, T.G., & McDonald, B.A. (1990). *Teach the mother and reach the child: Literacy across generations*. Geneva, Switzerland: International Bureau of Education.

Strauss, A. (1987). *Qualitative analysis for social scientists*. New York: Cambridge University Press.

Strauss, A., & Corbin, J. (1990). *Basics of qualitative research: Grounded theory procedures and techniques*. Newbury Park, CA: Sage.

Swadener, B.B. (1995). Children and families "at promise": Deconstructing the discourse of risk. In B.B. Swadener & S. Lubeck (Eds.), *Children and families "at promise": Deconstructing the discourse of risk* (pp. 17–49). Albany, NY: State University of New York Press.

Taylor, D. (1993). Family literacy: Resisting deficit models. *TESOL Quarterly, 27,* 550–553.

Taylor, D. (1997). *Many families, many literacies*. Portsmouth, NH: Heinemann.

Taylor, D., & Dorsey-Gaines, C. (1988). *Growing up literate: Learning from inner-city families*. Portsmouth, NH: Heinemann.

Teale, W.H. (1986). Home background and young children's literacy development. In W.H. Teale & E. Sulzby (Eds.), *Emergent literacy: Writing and reading* (pp. 173–206). Norwood, NJ: Ablex.

Valdés, G. (1996). *Con Respeto: Bridging the distances between culturally diverse families and schools*. New York: Teachers College Press.

Author Index

L

Langer, J., 2, 128
Lareau, A., 4–5, 109, 129

M

McDonald, B.A., 2, 131
Miles, M.B., 16–17, 130
Mishler, E.G., 12–14, 130
Moles, O.C., 112, 130
Moll, L.C., 6, 130
Mulhern, M., 6, 114, 131
Mullis, I., 2, 113–114, 128, 130

N

National Center for Children in
    Poverty, 114, 130

O

Owens, E.H., 113–114, 130

P

Paratore, J.R., 7–9, 11, 130
Paull, S., 2–3, 130
Phillips, G.W., 113–114, 130
Pittman, K., 113, 129
Popp, B., 7, 131
Potts, M.W., 2–3, 130

Q

Quintero, E., 6, 114, 130

R

Reading Excellence Act of 1998,
    1–2, 130
Rodriguez-Brown, F., 6, 114, 131

S

Seaman, D., 7, 130
Seidman, I.E., 12–14, 131
Shanahan, T., 6, 114, 131
Sloane, K., 2, 129
Snow, C.E., 110, 111, 131
Solís, J., 113, 114, 131
Sticht, T.G., 2, 131
Strauss, A., 16, 131
Swadener, B.B., 3–4, 131

T

Taylor, D., 3, 4, 5, 108–109, 131
Teale, W.H., 2, 131

V

Valdés, G., 3, 4, 110, 112, 131
Velarde, M.C., 6, 130

Subject Index

Note: Page references followed by *t* indicate tables. Those followed by *A, B, C, D, E,* or *F* indicate respective Appendices.

A–C

ACADEMIC SUCCESS OF CHILDREN. *See also* Intergenerational Literacy Project (ILP): barriers to home-school relationships, 110; book-reading experiences and, 2; economic influences of, 4–5, 109–110, 114; family and community literacy practices and, 3–4; funding programs to support, 1–2; of Latino children, 113–114; parental attitudes and, 2–3; parental education and, 2; parental involvement and, 2, 3–4, 6–7, 110–111; parental literacy and language skills and, 5–7; parental support of, 108–109; social inequalities and, 3–5

CHILDREN'S DEFENSE FUND, 114

CULTURAL CAPITAL, 5, 109–110

CULTURAL DIVERSITY. *See* immigrant families

E

EDUCATIONAL RESOURCES, access to and quality of, 113–114

ETHNICITIES. *See* immigrant families

EVEN START MODEL, 1

F

FAILURE IN SCHOOLS. *See* academic success of children

FAMILY INITIATIVE FOR ENGLISH LITERACY, 6–7

FAMILY LITERACY PROGRAMS, 114. *See also* specific programs; empowerment of parents by, 6; Family Initiative for English Literacy, 6–7; funding for, 1–2; Project FLAME, 6; responses to, 1–2, 3–4; as solution to underachievement in schools, 1

FEDERALLY FUNDED PROGRAMS, for family literacy, 1–2

FUNDING, for family literacy programs, 1–2

H

M–N

MINORITIES. *See also* immigrant families: children of color, 5; high school drop-out rates of, 113

NATIONAL CENTER FOR CHILDREN IN POVERTY, 114

NATIONAL CENTER FOR FAMILY LITERACY, 2–3

P

PACE/KENAN PROGRAMS, 2–3

PARENTING SKILLS, 3

PARENTS. *See also* Intergenerational Literacy Project (ILP): empowerment of, 6; life-coping skills for, 2; prompts for conversations with, 121*B*

POVERTY, 114

PROFILES, child and parent, 13*t*

PROJECT FLAME, 6

PROMPTS FOR CONVERSATIONS WITH CHILDREN, for Intergenerational Literacy Project (ILP), 128–129*E*

PROMPTS FOR CONVERSATIONS WITH PARENTS, for Intergenerational Literacy Project (ILP), 121*B*

PROMPTS FOR CONVERSATIONS WITH TEACHERS, for Intergenerational Literacy Project (ILP), 119–120*A*

Q–R

QUALITATIVE RESEARCH SOFTWARE, 16

READING EXCELLENCE ACT, 1998, 1

RESEARCH MATERIALS (ILP): learner intake form, 122–125*C*; literacy log, 126–127*D*; prompts for conversations with children, 128–129*E*; prompts for conversations with parents, 121*B*; prompts for conversations with teachers, 119–120*A*; working codes, 130–131*F*

RESEARCH SOFTWARE, qualitative, 16

S

SCHOOL PRACTICES, 110–111, 111–112

SCHOOL SUCCESS. *See* academic success of children

SOCIAL CAPITAL, 4–5, 109–110

SOCIAL INEQUALITIES, and academic success of children, 3–5

SOCIAL SKILLS, for children, 3

SOFTWARE, qualitative research, 16

T

TEACHERS, prompts for conversations with, 119–120*A*

U–W